Praise for *A New Harmony*

"*A New Harmony* is a theology that is at once a prayer, and a prayer that is at once a theology. John Philip Newell offers herein a deeply nondualistic theology that is authentically Christian but one that has also listened intently to Hindu traditions. The result is a vision of interrelatedness that is more fundamental than all the fragmentations that mark our age and the human heart. The tragic reality of rupture is not denied, but Newell is rooted in a tradition of divine immanence that refuses to give to brokenness the final word. Instead, we are invited into a new and at once ancient harmony, one in which we move and live and have our being. This wisdom can make us hale by making us whole, if we would but listen."–John J. Thatamanil, author, *The Immanent Divine: God, Creation, and the Human Predicament*

"John Philip Newell calls his unifying approach to Christianity 'new-ancient.' The 'ancient' he offers in this volume draws on the vast array of spiritual riches in our Christian tradition. The 'new' is as provocative and life-giving as the latest work from prophetic writers such as Rob Bell, Marcus Borg, and *Newsweek*'s Lisa Miller. All are engaged in global conversation about the pathway that lies ahead, not only for the world's two billion Christians, but for all of humanity and all of God's Creation." –David Crumm, editor, www.ReadTheSpirit.com

"This book represents what is becoming a new and abundant source for theology, although it is the oldest source of all—creation itself! How could we have missed what John Philip Newell now makes so obvious and so exciting?"–Richard Rohr, O.F.M., Center for Action and Contemplation

"John Philip Newell possesses three gifts of the Spirit that are too rarely found in the same person at the same time. He is able to see the divine wholeness in our clearly fractured reality. He is able to articulate that wholeness so that we can see it too. Finally, he is able to connect his vision to action so that we are able to follow him into the new harmony he describes so compellingly—and all without a shred of sentimentality. If you know John Philip, here is an opportunity to be with him again. If you do not know him, this is a grand place to start."
—Barbara Brown Taylor, author, *An Altar in the World*

"In these pages Celtic consciousness and scholarship once again awaken the heart and mind to what is real in religion, the everyday beauty and sacredness of things. Simply, but not simplistically, written, the author moves from dreams and everyday encounters to teachings from creation-centered mystics and today's scientific cosmology, offering the reader a spiritual ride of depth and exhilaration. He provides a radical challenge to the boredom that institutional religion so often elicits. With a book like this, religious history looks less bleak and spirituality much closer to home."—Matthew Fox, author, *Original Blessing*

"A gift with a catch to it! *A New Harmony* is another little gem of spiritual wisdom from John Philip Newell. Often autobiographical, always engaging, at this moment when hope seems to recede from our nation and our planet, these reflections invite us into a hope for the renewal of an ancient harmony."—Wendy Farley, author, *Tragic Vision: A Contemporary Theodicy*

A NEW HARMONY

A NEW HARMONY

The Spirit, the Earth, and the Human Soul

John Philip Newell

SAINT ANDREW PRESS
Edinburgh

First published in the UK in 2012 by
SAINT ANDREW PRESS
121 George Street
Edinburgh EH2 4YN

First published in the US by Jossey-Bass, a Wiley Imprint
989 Market Street, San Francisco, CA 94103-1741

Copyright © John Philip Newell, 2012
ISBN 978 0 86153 698 6
Kindle ISBN 978 0 86153 711 2

British Library Cataloguing in Publication Data
A catalogue record for this book is available from the British Library.

It is the publisher's policy to only use papers that are natural and recyclable and
that have been manufactured from timber grown in renewable, properly
managed forests. All of the manufacturing processes of the papers are expected
to conform to the environmental regulations of the country of origin.

Readers should be aware that Internet Web sites offered as citations and/or
sources for further information may have changed or disappeared between the
time this was written and when it is read.

Please note that any advice or strategies contained herein may not be suitable
for your personal situation. You should consult with a professional where
appropriate. Neither the publisher nor author shall be liable for any loss of
profit or any other commercial damages, including but not limited to special,
incidental, consequential, or other damages.

Printed and bound in the United Kingdom by
CPI Group (UK) Ltd, Croydon

CONTENTS

INTRODUCTION

I occasionally used to see Philip and Ali Newell on Iona during the time they were wardens of Iona Abbey. I didn't know them; I just recognized them when I saw them and greeted them. It was only in later years – really not all that long ago – that I began to get to know them.

From earliest childhood days the island of Iona has been my spiritual home. It's where my mother found faith when everything else in her life had been swept away, and it's where I was taken on holiday most summers. I learned to walk on one of the island's beaches, and I learned to love the Abbey, this church with its cluster of monastic buildings built once by Columba and his monks, and restored through the first decades of last century. In particular I loved the cloister. The darkness of the little stone corridors with the pillars opening onto the brightness of an unroofed square of grass. No-one ever suggested the idea to me, and I have no idea where the thought came from, but I firmly believed that this place was the centre of the earth.

In later years I came to think of Iona as a place on the edge. It takes a long time to reach from the centres, the places our contemporary society thinks of as important. It is two islands removed from the mainland.

Later still, and to this day, since I've come to study the island story more deeply, particularly in the 6th Century, at the time Columba brought the Christian story into being. Iona became again a centre point, at the meeting of all the sea roads between Scotland and Ireland. And so it exists today in my mind and heart, both an edge place and a centre point.

Philip Newell challenges so much of our easy, safe conventional Christianity, and as I was reading this new work I was reminded of the Iona of my heart: edge place and centre point. It made me think of my own faith, of how in so many ways it is kept in an edge place, where most likely it feels safest.

The faith of all people is being challenged today as a new quasi-religious agnosticism is born, a melding of the confidence of science and the result of the near nihilism of western society. What does it mean to believe? What does it mean for others to believe?

It is no longer possible to remain safe and unchallenged in an edge place. We are in danger whenever we think the piece of thinking we have come to make our own is the only truth. Philip Newell goes about the business of seeking out what is *shared* in this faith journey of ours – as Jews, Muslims, Hindus and Christians – rather than what divides us. He has been challenged particularly by the story of India, by the Christians who have gone not to impose their version of a western God on the country, but who have sought to listen honestly and humbly instead for the voice of God in India.

There are times we would do well to admit there is much we have to learn. We have to make new journeys – both out into the wider world and deeper into ourselves – to dig away the rubble and find God once more, in a new way or place. And it is not only about our re-discovering God; it is about allowing God to re-discover us, to re-awaken us to new light.

It is about both centre points and edge places. Our journeys are made in faith and with faith; it is not about relinquishing what lies at the heart of our Christian soul-set, but rather about being open to learning and listening, about being willing to see clearly and look out rather than only always in.

Kenneth Steven

PROLOGUE

The word *kosmos* in ancient Greek means "a harmony of parts." In the classical world, everything in the universe was viewed as moving in relation to everything else. This ancient understanding of the cosmos is being born afresh today in radically new ways. We are realizing that the whole of reality is one. In nearly every dimension of life—whether economic or religious, scientific or political—there is a growing awareness of earth's essential interrelatedness. This new-ancient way of seeing is radically challenging us to see ourselves as connected with everything else that exists. And it means that any true vision of reality must also be a cosmology, a way of relating the parts to the whole, of seeing our distinct journeys in relation to the one journey of the universe.

A few years ago, my wife and I went on pilgrimage to the Sinai. There were four of us—Mousa, our desert guide; Hamda, our Bedouin cook; and Ali and me. We slept under the open skies at night, and every morning before sunrise we would hear the crackling of the breakfast fire prepared by Hamda. Somehow in the barren landscape of the Sinai she would find dead roots of desert bushes for kindling in order to freshly bake us unleavened bread for breakfast. Then the great fire of the rising sun would blaze over the eastern horizon to warm our night-chilled bodies.

On the last day, we made our way to Mount Sinai, climbed half of it on camel back, then hiked the centuries-old carved steps of stone to the peak for sunset. No one else was with us on the summit as the setting sun threw its red radiance across the great range of desert peaks. We visited the three shrines of prayer that honor the disclosure of the Holy Presence in this place—one Jewish, one Christian, one Muslim—and descended the mountain in silence. The moon was fat, and its whiteness shone off the desert sand, throwing moon shadows from the high rocks and the sharp turns of our descent. At the mountain base, we approached the fourth-century St. Catherine's Monastery where we were to spend the night. In the moonlight it looked as it might have looked at any time in its sixteen centuries. And although it held within its walls a Christian monastic community, a burning bush revered by Jewish pilgrims, and a mosque prayed in by Muslims from around the world, under the moon's light it looked as one.

Carl Jung speaks of "moon-like consciousness," a way of seeing in which we more readily perceive oneness than differentiation.[1] When I walk under the light of the moon, I am at times almost speechless with wonder. Under the moonlight, life's edges are not so sharply defined. The boundaries are less distinct. In the daylight, in contrast, I have much more to say because I am seeing everything more analytically. The parts are easily distinguished from the whole. Moon-like consciousness is ours in dream life and meditative practice as well, as it is in some of our earliest memories of childhood when we glimpsed the "Golden World," as Robert Johnson calls it, the world of unitary vision rather than separation.[2] What has happened to our moon-like consciousness?

The next day at St. Catherine's Monastery, under the scorching heat of the midday sun, I noticed Jewish pilgrims scolding their children for tearing off bits of the burning bush, Muslim attendants at the mosque barking out instructions for visitors to take off their shoes, and Christian monks avidly selling tickets so that pilgrims might view the ancient holy manuscripts. This was no longer moon-like consciousness. This was seeing by the light of day.

The reality is that we need both. We need moon-like consciousness and sun-like consciousness, even if the latter has a way of highlighting the crude nature of our separations. We need the distinct wisdoms that underlie our different cultures and traditions. But without moon-like consciousness, without remembering that our human journey began as one and that the birth of the earth and its unfolding life are one, we will splinter further and further into fragmented parts in which we dangerously forget the whole. Sun-like consciousness alone, with its primary focus on differentiation—whether between individuals or nations or species—has proved to be inadequate. It is not enough. But today a new-ancient way of seeing is being born, a moon-like consciousness in which we are remembering also our oneness. How do we translate this awareness into action?

Being newly aware of life's essential oneness does not mean that we should downplay the unique treasure of our various wisdom traditions. My experience of working closely with teachers from other religious households leads me to believe that we should dig more deeply into our distinct treasure troves in order to offer wisdom to one another. We can serve the new awareness most effectively not by watering down the distinctness of our traditions but by bringing our varied gifts to serve one another and our shared journey—the journey of the earth and the human soul.

A New Harmony: The Spirit, the Earth, and the Human Soul is written from within the Christian household. It is an attempt to serve the emerging awareness of life's essential oneness by drawing in part on the ancient wisdom of Jesus. But it is not a book only for Christians. My desire is to communicate across the boundaries of religion and race that have separated us and to honor our distinct inheritances by serving what is deeper still—the oneness of our origins and the oneness of earth's destiny.

The book follows a threefold pattern. In the first part, I explore the ancient harmony that is deep in the matter of the universe, the essential interwovenness of all things. Everything, whether the expanding light of distant galaxies or humanity's inner light of mind and consciousness, carries within itself the life of the universe's shared beginning. Second, I explore the brokenness of our harmony, whether as individuals and families or as nations and species. Knowing and naming the extent and depth of our disharmony is essential to finding the way forward. Confronting our brokenness, individually and together, is integral to the hope for healing. And third, I ask how we can be part of a new harmony. What is the cost, both personal and collective, of releasing life's essential oneness in radically new and transformative ways?

One of the most precious teachings in the Celtic Christian world is the memory of John the Beloved leaning against Jesus at the Last Supper. It was said of him that he therefore heard the heartbeat of God. He became a symbol of the practice of listening—listening deep within ourselves, listening deep within one another, listening deep within the body of the earth for the beat of the Holy. Do we know, each one of us, that we are bearers of the sacred beat of life? Do we know that we can honor that beat in one another and in all things? And do we know that it is this combination—of knowing that we are bearers of Presence and of choosing to honor the Presence in one another—that holds the key to transformation in our lives and world?

To listen for the heartbeat of God is to listen both within the vastness of the universe and within the intimacy of our own hearts. And it is to know these distinct ways of listening as essentially one, as two aspects of the same posture of consciousness. The deeper we move in the mystery of our soul, the closer we come to hearing the beat of the cosmos; and the more we expand our awareness into the vastness of the universe, the closer we come to knowing the unbounded Presence at the heart of our being and every being. As new science is teaching us, the microcosm and the macrocosm are one. Our lives are part of the cosmos, and the cosmos

is part of us. The life of humanity is not an appendix or an
exception to the universe. It is a unique expression of the
universe. And each of us carries the essence of the cosmos
within us.

In the late 1980s, my wife and I moved to the Western
Isles of Scotland to take up the wardenship of Iona Abbey,
a modern-day religious community committed to nonvio-
lence and justice. Since the sixth century, Iona has been a
place of pilgrimage to which countless numbers of men and
women have come seeking new beginnings in their lives
and nations. Today hundreds of thousands visit the island
every year and pray for peace. Early in our time on the
island, I overheard a profound conversation between our
two eldest children. They were still young enough to be
profound! Brendan, five years of age, was asking our seven-
year-old Rowan, "Where is God?" to which she replied,
"God is in our hearts." Brendan sat looking perplexed by
this answer and then, after a moment of silence, said, "So,
God goes beat, beat, beat."

When I am asked to say one thing about spirituality, I
often quote my Brendan. God goes beat, beat, beat. God,
the very heartbeat of life, the Soul within our soul, the
Presence without whom there would be no present. But my
Brendan now as a young man is often unable to hear the
beat at the heart of life. In his late teens he suffered a severe
mental breakdown that holds him in a type of imprison-
ment to anxiety and at times paranoia. The longer we have
lived with mental illness within us as a family, the more I
have come to believe that Brendan's illness is not his, in a
limited sense. It is certainly his on a daily basis as he battles

fear in almost every moment and every relationship. But it is not limitedly his. It is ours, ours as a family but also ours as a society and as a world today. Through Brendan we have come to know other young men who similarly suffer from anxiety. These are sensitive and often artistic young men. They are manifesting our illness. They are exhibiting symptoms of the fear that drives our nations, our societies, our lifestyles. And I have come to believe that Brendan will not be truly well until we are well, and that we will not be truly well until Brendan and others like him are well. Our healing belongs inextricably together.

We live in the midst of a new consciousness of life's interrelatedness. And this awareness relates both to life's essential oneness and to life's shared brokenness. Like never before in the history of humanity, we are becoming aware that what we do to a part we do to the whole, that the parts will not be well as long as the whole is neglected, and that the whole will not be well if the parts are neglected. We know that it is meaningless to speak of being truly well as parents if our children are unwell. We know that we cannot claim true wellness for our nation as long as other nations are suffering. And we know that the human species can in no sense be considered healthy when the body of the earth is deeply infected. Wellness is found not in isolation but in relationship.

This emerging awareness can be described as a new Pentecost on a vast and unprecedented scale. It can be described as a fresh outpouring of Spirit. Just as Hebrew Scripture begins with a description of the Wind of God hovering over the chaotic deep at the beginning of time to bring forth creation in its oneness, that same Spirit is hovering over the depths of the human soul today to bring forth a consciousness of life's oneness that we could never before have imagined. Similarly, at the beginning of the Acts of the Apostles in Christian Scripture there is the story of the Holy Spirit breathing a new passion for oneness into the early followers of Jesus, so that on Pentecost day in Jerusalem, they spoke a language that could be understood by every nation. That same Spirit is breathing a new vision of oneness into our awareness today. And it transcends the narrow boundaries that our nations and religions have tried to place around us. A new and vast Pentecost is stirring in the human soul. How will we serve it?

This awareness of earth's essential oneness has been prophetically led by new science. David Bohm in his seminal work, *Wholeness and the Implicate Order*, along with many other new physicists, has enabled us to see that everything that has come into being in space and time was implicated in the first moment, in that tiny pinprick of light that exploded forth into the expanding universe. Everything is an explication of what was implicated in that initial moment. Similarly, new psychology, in the teachings of Ken Wilbur and others, has enabled us to conceive that everything in the universe holds within itself a type of physical memory of the first moment, so inextricably linked are all things.

In many ways, new science has only been catching up with the ancient insights of humanity's great spiritual traditions, which all along have been saying that we come from the One and that we will be well to the extent that we reconnect with the One. In the Celtic world as early as the ninth century, John Scotus Eriugena taught that all things were made "together and at once."[3] He was not saying that all things became visible at the same time. He was saying that all things are hidden in "the secret folds of nature" waiting for the time of their manifestation.[4] So much are we one that everything that unfolds within us and within the universe was present in embryo in the first moment. We carry the essence of all things within us. And all things carry the essence of our being within them.

If the deep spirit of our age is this new awareness of life's essential oneness, if the new Pentecost is leading us into what David Bohm calls a "non-fragmentary world view," then what are we to make of the deep fragmentations of the world today?[5] What is it that is driving humanity to the precipitous edge of self-destruction, more dangerous than anything history has witnessed? At the heart of our fragmentations, whether as nations and wisdom traditions or as races and societies, are various forms of fundamentalism. By fundamentalism I do not mean simply religious fundamentalism, although I certainly include that. By fundamentalism I mean any system that perceives reality in hard-edged terms, that boxes in truth with four fixed walls of definition. Fundamentalism says that what the rest of humanity needs is inside these tight boundaries of truth. What humanity needs is *our* religious dogma. What all nations need is *our* ideal of democracy. What the world needs is the supremacy of *our* race. What people in committed relationship need is *our* pattern of sexual orientation. And the list goes on and on.

At the heart of such hard-edged boundaries is fear. Fundamentalism has always reared its head at times of significant change. Think, for instance, of the extreme fundamentalisms that came to expression in the Christian household in the nineteenth century—biblical literalism at one end of the spectrum and papal infallibility at the other. Both systems were driven by fear. Both felt threatened in an era of great transition, in the wake of evolutionary thought in which life was no longer viewed in fixed terms but as forever unfolding, and in the wake of higher literary and historical criticism in which it seemed that the authoritative texts of our Christian tradition were under assault. Fundamentalism reacted to the spirit of the age by further hardening its lines of definition and by trying to impose the rigid boundaries of the past on the emerging future.

We too live in the midst of enormous change. We too are being invited to view life in radically new terms—to see all things as essentially interwoven, to see life as one. And the fundamentalist within us, within the household of our nation, within the household of our religion, and even within the household of our own families and hearts, is reacting in fear. The fundamentalist within knows that we are being called to change. And at some level, fundamentalism knows that it will be a costly change. If we are one, then we are going to have to change the way we view ourselves as nations, as wisdom traditions, as families, and as individuals. If we are one, then we are going to have to radically change the way we live with the earth and one another.

We live at a costly moment. The question is, what type of cost will it be? Will it be the cost of transformation in which we reshape our lives and relationships, both collectively and individually, to serve the new Pentecost? Or will it be the cost of further and further fragmentation in which we take ourselves and earth's species toward destruction?

A comprehensive change of consciousness is coming. Something new is happening among us. And in the midst of something new being born, something old is dying. This expresses itself in countless realms of life, from communications to commerce to cuisine. It is manifesting itself also in the life of religion throughout the world, including the Christian household. In many parts of the Western world, Christianity as we have known it is in a state of collapse—even seismic collapse. What is the new thing that is waiting to be born? And what is the old thing that is disappearing before our very eyes?

One of the great prophets of the modern soul was Carl Jung, the founder of analytical psychology. Even as a boy he had prophetic intuitions, although it was not until adulthood that he was able to find expression for many of them. In *Memories, Dreams, Reflections,* Jung recounts how as a schoolboy in 1887 he was walking past the great cathedral in Basel, Switzerland, with its shining new spire, when an image from the unconscious began to stir within him. At first he was so horrified by the image that he tried pushing it back down into the unconscious. But it kept insisting on coming forth. Finally, when it fully emerged in his consciousness, he realized that what he saw above the spire of the cathedral was the throne of God. And descending from the throne was "an enormous turd" that smashed into the spire and broke apart the walls of the cathedral.[6]

We are living in the midst of the great turd falling! And it is not only falling. It has already smashed into the spire of Western Christianity. I for one am a lover of our medieval cathedrals. And I believe we may be able to find ways of integrating the artistry and religious imagination of our past into the new thing that is being born. But as long as we allow our spires to give the impression that God is primarily above and beyond the earth, in opposition to what is deepest in creation and in the body of the human mystery, then our spires are going to crumble.

We live at the end of an era. As Robert Johnson says, the symbol of "up" is changing to "down."[7] We need a new mythology. If we are to retain our spires as symbols that point to the otherness of God, we need at the same time to develop symbols that point to the withinness of God. As well as upward spires we need something like downward spires, vessels that hold the holy rather than simply pointing away to the Holy. We need to create, or reclaim, images like the holy wells that lie beneath the very foundations of many of our medieval cathedrals, to remind us that the deeper we move into the mystery of matter, the closer we come to the One from whom all things are born. Meister Eckhart in the fourteenth century held this tension in balance when he said that "height and depth are the same thing."[8] Transcendence and immanence belong together. The One who is beyond us is at the same time the very Ground of our being.

Over the last five years, I have watched my second daughter, Kirsten, intuitively discover through dance form what many of us are longing for today, the relationship between the earth and sacredness. Kirsten was reared in the West and as a little girl studied ballet. She now lives in the East as a student of Indian dance. In Western ballet she was forever leaving the ground and standing on tiptoe, reaching to the heavens. In the sacred dance of India, Bharata Natyam, she is flat-footed with bent knees, her feet sometimes pounding the earth with great force to release its sacred energy. In my daughter I see the human soul's search for wholeness. In Kirsten's case, it was her body that told her that the other half of her soul was to be found in India. Where is the search for wholeness taking us today, and to what shall we listen, in our longings both to reach to heaven and to stand firmly on the earth?

Our word *religion* is derived from the Latin *religare*, which means "to bind back together." The tragedy is that so much religion has been used to tear apart, to divorce heaven from earth, spirit from matter, one people from another. Holiness has been associated with a separation from the deepest energies of the human body or a being set apart from the rest of humanity. What we now need, says Jung, is "the illumination of a holy and whole-making spirit."[9] The new holiness into which we are being invited is the holiness of wholeness, of coming back into relationship with the earth and what is deepest in the human soul. Our English words *holy* and *whole* are derived from the same root, from the Anglo-Saxon *hale*, meaning "health." To have split holiness from wholeness is the neurosis at the heart of much of our religiosity, of pretending that we can be well by pursuing paths of separation, of imagining that we can be whole by seeking heaven at the expense of earth.

The Spirit, says Jung, is "a complexio oppositorum," a bringing together again of what has been torn apart, a marriage of what has been considered opposite—heaven and earth, East and West, spirit and matter, the feminine and the masculine, night and day, the sun and the moon, the conscious and the unconscious, the heart and the head, spirituality and sexuality, the one and the many, my own well-being and the well-being of my neighbor, the rights of humanity and the life of every species.[10] The new holiness is wholeness. The new Pentecost is a conjoining of opposites. Without it we will not be holy. Without it we will not be whole.

For many today, including members of my own family, the word God is difficult to use. It is almost irredeemable because of its association with the spire, with a pointing away to the sacred rather than pointing deep within to the Ground of Life. I understand the struggle. We need to be creative in our use of language to find images that will deeply serve this point in time, words that are born from the new awareness of life's essential oneness and that free us from the tragic separations of heaven and earth, spirit and matter, the masculine and the feminine. I also believe it is important to use the word God if we can, but to use it as one among many names for the Holy. It will enable us to hold the past and the present in relationship, to live in a creative tension between the new thing that is being born and the old thing from which we have come, to live in a spirit of gratitude to our religious inheritance as well as to criticize its limitations. The Sufi Muslim tradition of the ninety-nine names of God has much to teach us. It is based on a belief that the true name of the Holy One is the hundredth name but that no one knows that name, for it is unspeakable.

As we bring to our spirituality a posture of listening, listening to the essential oneness of the universe, placing our ear close to the heart of the earth and the heart of the human soul, what is it we will hear? Julian of Norwich, the fourteenth-century mystic, says that we are not simply made by God. We are made "of God."[11] This simple but radical statement holds enormous implications. It means that we are not fashioned by a distant Creator, made out of nothing from afar, as it were. Rather we are born from the womb of the One, made of the substance of oneness. This is why Julian likes to refer to God as Mother, as well as Father, because she sees us and all things as coming forth from the heart of the One, as carrying within ourselves the essence of our Source.

What does it mean to say that we are made of God rather than simply by God? In part it is to say that holy wisdom is deep within us, deeper than the ignorance of what we have done. Sacred creativity is at the core of our being, deeper than any barrenness in our lives or relationships. The divine passion for what is just and right is our true heart's desire, deeper than the apathies and falsenesses that have disabled us. And above all else it is to say, as Julian does, that the "love-longing" of God is at the core of our being, deeper than any fear or hatred that holds us in separation.[12] We are made of the One. Deep within us, amid our differentiations as individuals and nations and species, is the desire for oneness. This holy longing is found not only in the human soul but in the soul of the universe, at the heart of every-thing that has being. We are not an exception to the universe. We are an expression of the universe. Our longings are a unique manifestation of the universe's longings. In listening to the depths of life, within our lives and within every life, we will hear the longings of the One that are deeper than the fears that divide us.

In the late 1990s, we lived as a family in Portsmouth, England. Ali and I were part of developing a spirituality center in the heart of the city. The Church of England had provided us with an old unused vicarage set in a big walled-in garden. This green, growing space, surrounded by the crowded city's hard concrete, became in time a sanctuary and a symbol of well-being in which to pray with others and to teach. As we turned over the earth with our hands, which were sometimes cut with the briars and broken glass of years of neglect and abandonment, we felt within us the longing to tend again what has been forsaken—the garden of our shared beginnings, the sacred ground of life's oneness.

The few birds who chose to live in the heart of the city found their way to our Portsmouth garden with its trees and openness and water. Often I would wake at dawn to the sound of a pair of mourning doves cooing at the top of our chimney. One day as I worked at my desk, I became aware of a sound of struggle in the chimney. I was busy, working to deadline, and did not want to be interrupted, but the sound came closer and closer. Finally I realized I had to do something about it. So I got down on my hands and knees in front of the fireplace, which years before had been sealed off, and began pulling out the pieces of mid-twentieth-century newspaper that had been used to block off the chimney. Decades of dirt and dust were clouding the study. And I became aware of a growing anxiety within myself—*What am I going to do with this creature when it arrives?*

I placed my hand up into the flue and felt the bird. When I touched her she became entirely still, frozen with fear. Gently I drew her down into the hearth of the open fireplace. And there she sat in my hands. It was one of the beautiful white mourning doves that sang to me each dawn. But now she was covered with soot and traumatized with fear. I took her out into the garden and placed her high on a wall, but still she sat stunned. I went back into the study to get on with my work, and an hour later returned to the garden. There she was, still in a state of shock. But this time as I approached she flew, and as she flew the soot fell off. In the midday sun she became again an image of beauty and of freedom.

For days after this event, I was haunted by the memory of the mourning dove. It was not the memory of her stuck in the chimney that haunted me. It was the sight of her sitting on the wall, traumatized by her fall and covered with soot. I realized she represented something in me, something in us. It had been unawareness that led to her topple into the chimney. And sitting on the wall, even though strictly speaking she was free from her fall, she was not yet truly herself. She was the same mourning dove who sang to me each day at dawn, but she would not recover her true form and beauty until she flew again. How are the traumas of our falls and fears to be healed? And how are we to set one another free? How can we be part of releasing wholeness and beauty again in our lives and world?

Too often in our Western Christian household, and in ways that have affected our wider culture as well, we have been given the impression that soot is our essence. The doctrine of original sin has dominated the landscape of much of our teaching. It has given us the impression that what is deepest in us is contrary to the One from whom we have come. And teachers who have opposed the doctrine of original sin, like Pelagius in the early Celtic world, have been accused of naivete, of insufficiently recognizing our capacity for wrong and division. Even today such accusations against Pelagius prevail in most of our Western Christian seminaries. And usually these accusations are made without any firsthand study of Pelagius's writings; sometimes there is even denial that such writings exist. Pelagius taught that at the heart of our being is the beauty of God and the wisdom of God. He also taught, however, that we are infected by sin, so deeply infected that we need the medicine of grace if we are to be well, if we are to access again the deep intuitions and longings of our being. Like the mourning dove, we have been traumatized by our fall. We need help. We need "the good of nature," says Pelagius, "and the good of grace."[13]

Nature and grace are both sacred gifts, and they both come to us through the most essential relationships of life. We are born from the earth and from our mother's womb. This is our origin, or in Latin our *natus*, our nature. It is pure gift, and it is sacred. The gift of grace, which is awakened in us through compassion, is not opposed to the gift of our nature. Rather it restores us to the heart of our nature. It reconnects us to the love-longings of God at the core of our being, our yearnings for oneness and relationship. It is grace that will free us from the unnaturalness of what we are doing to one another and to the earth.

In this new Pentecost, we are being invited to bring our gifts of nature and grace to one another so that together we may be complete. What are the treasures we can offer each other as individuals and families, as communities and nations, as wisdom traditions and as species? In the Christian tradition, our greatest treasure is the wisdom of Jesus. Yet many of us have forgotten how to access this gift for the sake of the world because we have been appalled at the way in which Christianity has arrogantly placed itself above other traditions.

The word *revelation* is from the Latin *revelare*, which means "to lift the veil." Jesus is our great gift of revelation. He lifts the veil, but it is not to show us an exclusive truth. It is to show us the most inclusive of truths, that we and all things are made of God. We can share Jesus humbly with the world. We can offer our treasure in love. In the earliest centuries, he was described as our "memory," the one who reminds us of what we have forgotten, awakening us to who we truly are, made of the One.[14] In the Celtic world, he was spoken of as "our epiphany," disclosing to us what is deepest in the life of all things, the sacredness of everything that has being.[15] And in the modern world, he has been described as revealing the hidden "ground-life" of our being, bringing to consciousness the treasure that lies buried in our depths.[16] Our gift is not opposed to the wisdom of other traditions. It is given to serve the wisdom of other traditions. We do not have to compete with one another. We can complete one another.

We live in the midst of a unique moment. Thomas Berry calls it a "moment of grace."[17] It is a decisive moment in which we are being offered a new-ancient way of seeing with which to transform the fragmentations of our lives and world back into relationship. But if we miss this moment, choosing instead to continue our patterns of wronging the earth and one another, there will be a degradation of life on this planet like none we have ever known. What will we choose? Which path will we follow?

In Memoriam

Jane Blaffer Owen

(1915–2010)

a prophet of New Harmony

PART ONE

THE ANCIENT HARMONY

CHAPTER 1

EVERY BUSH
IS BURNING

In 1990, Harry Underhill, the nephew of the English
mystic Evelyn Underhill, invited me to India. I was at
that stage warden of Iona Abbey in the Western Isles
of Scotland. Harry felt that the Iona Community could do
with some exposure to the East. I met him in London, and
we flew together to Madras. Our plan was to travel further
south in Tamil Nadu, to the ashram of the great Benedictine
monk Bede Griffiths, who had devoted much of his life to
the marriage of East and West.

On my first night in India, I had a dream in which I
was drinking vodka with Mikhail Gorbachev. In what at first
seemed a convivial atmosphere, we were knocking back
shots of vodka together. After the third round, however, I
noticed a chemical residue at the bottom of my glass. I was
being drugged. When I woke up I realized in part what the
dream was about. In traveling to the East for the first time,
there was some uncertainty in me about what I would
encounter. I was still a good Western boy. I had been trained
for the Church of Scotland ministry at New College in the
University of Edinburgh. Everything about my religious

history and philosophical training had led me to look to the
transcendent for God and to the mind for wisdom. And here
I was entering the East, the world of immanence and the
unconscious.

Mikhail Gorbachev is not exactly an Eastern guru. He
did, however, represent otherness to me, a world beyond
the defined boundaries of the West. Gorbachev at that
moment was in the midst of a revolution of thought. The
Berlin Wall separating East and West had come down two
months earlier. And as leader of the Soviet Union, a political
system based on fixed ideologies and doctrinaire structures,
Gorbachev was teaching *perestroika* ("restructuring") and
glasnost ("openness"). He represented the desire to open a
system that had been closed and to restructure it through
dialogue rather than doctrine.

I was anxious about entering the East. It felt like a
strange land to me. My Western education had trained me
to suspect Indian mysticism. It was too subjective. Part of
me feared that I would be deluded by drinking at the well
of Eastern spirituality. Carl Jung says that in India "one gets
pushed back into the unconscious."[1] That was my fear.
Dream life and the unconscious represented for me a world
of delusion. To open to it was to run the risk of being
flooded by unreality. I had been taught that truth was primarily outside myself, to be accessed through the intellect
and through propositional truths. And Western Christianity,
with its doctrine of original sin, had given me the impression that what was deepest in me was opposed to God. Here
in the East, I was about to encounter the opposite. I was
about to be encouraged to draw from the deep wellsprings

of my being and to open to the unconscious as a true channel of perception.

Meister Eckhart, the fourteenth-century Christian mystic, says that God is "everything" that is and God is "nothing" that is.[2] God is the Life within all life, to be found at the heart of all that has being—within the light of the rising sun, within the early morning breeze, within the waking consciousness of our minds and bodies every day. God is the Immanent One, everything that is. And at the same time, God is the Transcendent One, nothing that is. God is always more and other than the light of the heavens, the elements of earth, the spiritual and physical energies of the breath we breathe. The greatness of our Western religious inheritance is that we have been taught that God is nothing that is. God is purely transcendent. The East, in contrast, has never forgotten that God is everything that is. God is immanent.

My first visit to India turned out to be a great blessing in my life. It was both a perestroika and a glasnost. It restructured me, radically reorienting my way of seeing. And it opened me, to the East with its ancient wisdom as well as to the inner world of the unconscious. Such was India's blessing in my life that in the years to come I would draw heavily on its teachings and, even more important, on its prayerful meditative disciplines. And it was to lead me eventually to encourage my second daughter to go to the East and study.

In 2007, our Kirsten decided to train in Bangalore. She enrolled in the Attakalari School of Movement and Art to study a combination of Indian sacred dance and Western contemporary movement. I accompanied Kirsten to India for her first week to make sure she settled in all right. Bangalore, like all Indian cities, is full of color and scent and sound. All day long, and sometimes all night long too, one's senses are bombarded—by the ceaseless honking of horns on crowded streets, the smell of cow dung and curries, and the brilliant array of saris that adorn even the poorest women of India.

We delicate Westerners require more space than what Indian cities typically afford, so on most days Kirsten and I would seek a few hours of sanctuary in the Lal Bagh Gardens at the heart of Bangalore. I have always been struck in India by how willing people are to engage in conversation with total strangers. On busy streets and crowded buses, I have met Indians eager to communicate, not just about the weather and cricket but about philosophical and religious themes.

One day as we sat in the Lal Bagh Gardens, we were approached by an elderly Indian gentleman. He greeted us kindly and entered into conversation. After a few pleasantries, in which I learned that he was a retired banker, he said with a gentle sideways wagging of his head, "I have one question for you. Who are you?" I sensed that he was not asking me what my name was, but, wanting to feel my way into the conversation, I said, "My name is John Philip." To which he replied, still kindly nodding his head from side to side, "I was not asking you what your name was. I was asking who are you?" So I said to him, "I come from the same One you come from." This pleased him well enough that he proceeded with our discussion, in which he expounded for me the heart of Hindu wisdom. He spoke of the Self within all selves and of true self-knowledge as consisting of an awareness that our selves are rooted in the One who is at the heart of all life. He then said, with an even more emphatic wagging of his head, "I must be going now, but I have one final thing to say to you. You are God. And until you realize you are God, you will not be wise, you will not be happy, and you will not be free. Namaste." And off he went. Since then I have often wondered when I will have such a conversation in the Edinburgh Royal Botanic Gardens with a retired Scottish banker!

How do we interpret such Eastern wisdom? For most of us in the Western world, it requires a lot of interpretation because in the East, God is everything that is, whereas in the West, God is nothing that is. One of the most emphatic things to be said about the Indian banker's words to me is that he was not addressing my ego. He was addressing the essential depth in me that is also his true depth and the true depth of everything that has being. He was pointing to the Ground of my being, to the Self within all selves, to the One in whom all life is rooted.

Meister Eckhart says that "God is not found in the soul by adding anything but by a process of subtraction."[3] We do not need to add anything to our depths to find the One. We do, however, need to subtract our separating ego if we are to find the One who is the Ground of our being. We do not need to invoke a foreign Presence into our life. We do, however, need to die to the pretense that our ego is the ultimate center of our lives, or that the ego of our nation should be served as the defining center of international relationships, or that the ego of the human species should be the sole focus of the earth's purpose and journey.

Eckhart says that the person who has learned to pray "the will" be done is the pure presence of God among us.[4] Eckhart also prays "thy will be done" to express the otherness of God and the essence of personhood at the heart of the sacred. But by using the definite article "the," Eckhart is underlining that there is only one true will at the heart of all things, for we and all things are made of God. Although we may live tragically removed from the heart of our being, deep within us and deep within the universe is the will of God, the holy longing for oneness. The person who has learned to pray "the will" be done, who has died to his or her separating ego, is a redeeming embodiment of the One. And this One is to be found in all things not by addition but by subtraction. To touch a man or woman who has done the work of subtracting the dividing self, says Eckhart, is to "touch God."[5]

Having doubted whether I would ever have a conversation in the Edinburgh Botanic Gardens that would compare with the Lal Bagh Gardens conversation in India, I was in fact recently surprised by the gift of such a moment. A young Sikh Indian asked to meet me in Edinburgh. We walked in the Royal Botanic Gardens just behind our family flat. He had read one of my books and was puzzled by my description of God as "I am." "Who is this 'I am'?" he asked. I told him the story from the Hebrew Scripture of Moses encountering the Living Presence in a bush that was burning without being consumed. And of how when Moses asked for the name of God, the response was not "I am this" or "I am that," but simply "I am who I am" or "I will be what I will be" (Exodus 3:14). I am the One who is beyond definition or boundary, the One who is and without whom nothing would be. Having offered such a thorough answer to the question, I was surprised when my friend looked at me as if I had missed the point. He then said to me kindly, his head gently wagging from side to side, "But we are 'I am.' "

We need the wisdom of the East. We need to keep being reminded that the Holy One is not only nothing that is but also everything that is, that God is not only Other but also Ground, not only transcendent but also immanent. And at this point in time, we need especially to be hearing that the universe is "I am," that the Sacred Presence deep within us is also deep within the mystery of the universe. One of the relationships that will help remind us of this truth is our relationship with the East. I am grateful to my Indian Sikh brother. At the same time, I am still waiting for such a conversation with a retired Scottish banker!

New science now speaks of being able to detect the sound of the beginning in the universe. It vibrates within the matter of everything that has being. Here again new science is echoing the ancient wisdom of spiritual insight. In the twelfth century, Hildegard of Bingen taught that the sound of God resonates "in every creature."[6] It is "the holy sound," she says, "which echoes through the whole creation."[7] If we are to listen for the One from whom we have come, it is not away from creation that we are to turn our ears; it is not away from the true depths of our being that we are to listen. It is rather to the very heart of all life that we are to turn our inner attention. For then we will hear that the deepest sound within us is the deepest sound within one another and within everything that has being. We will hear that the true harmony of our being belongs to the universe and that the true harmony of the universe belongs to us. That, says Hildegard, is why when we hear certain pieces of music "we breathe deeply and sigh."[8] For at such moments we are hearing the sound of our beginnings. And we are hearing that everything arises from that sacred sound.

Last year I had a dream in which I heard the sound of God. At first it seemed like a single flow of breath in which everything in the universe was being carried along. When I later woke, I realized that what I was hearing was similar to what my Jewish brother Rabbi Nahum had taught me about the name of God. The sacred name, which to a faithful Jew is unspeakable because it is the name of the Holy One, is represented by the tetragrammaton YHWH. In the Christian household, we pronounce it "Yahweh" or "Jehovah." It is the name "I am" or "I will be what I will be" that was disclosed in the story of Moses and the burning bush. But Rabbi Nahum explained to me that if somehow we were able to pronounce the four Hebrew consonants represented by YHWH, they would sound like the flow of breath.

To begin with, that was what I was hearing in my dream, a sound of breath in which everything in the cosmos was flowing. It then became more like a river, a flow in which I and all things were being carried. I was intertwined with many others whom I did not know. Our arms and legs were wrapped around each other's in an ecstasy of oneness.

And in the dream I began to speak in an unknown tongue, in an ecstatic utterance. I cannot reproduce the sound, but what I was saying was something like, "Bala cura delva Einstein . . . sera tora ulva Einstein"!

Why "Einstein"? Why was my unconscious throwing up his name in this river of life? Part of Albert Einstein's genius was his development of the General Theory of Relativity in which he enabled us to see that everything exists in relationship. Everything in the universe is to be understood in relation to, or relative to, everything else. He saw that space does not exist in and by itself. It is only a way of describing the distance between the differentiations of what has emerged in the life of the cosmos. Similarly, time does not exist in any absolute sense. It is simply a way of measuring the change that occurs in anything that has been born in the universe's life.

The timing of a dream is always significant. The unconscious is inviting us through the particularity of our lives to become aware of something we are not yet fully conscious of. The dream of the river of life, in which everything is interwoven, occurred the morning that our Kirsten left Scotland for India. This time she was leaving, in a sense, for good. This time she was leaving to take up a new life in India, to be married and to devote herself more deeply to the sacred dance of her adopted country. Ali and I were delighted for her. We were also heartbroken at the thought of losing her from Scotland.

The ecstatic dream was telling me that there is no such thing as absolute separation in space and time. There is no such thing as being truly severed from one another and from those we love. We would not really be separated from Kirsten. We would only be distanced by this thing called space. Who are the people whose absence we grieve in our lives? What are the homelands from which we feel cut off? There is no such thing as ultimate separation between one part of the universe and another, between the well-being of the human species and earth's other species, between the life of one nation and the rest of the world. We and all people, we and those who have gone before us, we and all creatures, we and the universe are traveling together in one river of life. We carry each other within us. And the universe carries us within itself.

The ninth-century Irish teacher John Scotus Eriugena liked to play with words. He taught that the Greek word *theos*, meaning "God," is derived from the Greek verb *theo*, which means "to flow" or "to run."[9] God, he said, is the One who runs or flows through all things. If the subterranean flow of God were somehow dammed up or stopped, all things would cease to exist. God is not simply a dimension of life, into relationship with which we may choose or choose not to move. God is the very essence of life, the River in which everything is born, the Flow without which there would be no flow. Kenneth White, the Scottish poet, builds on Eriugena's playful etymology by saying that God is the "glow-flow," the glistening river that runs through the heart of all things.[10] And the invitation is not simply to analyze the flow but to dive more deeply into the flow, and to know that we are part of it.

David Bohm, the new physicist, speaks of the life of the universe as one continuous flow. It is what he calls an

"Undivided Wholeness in Flowing Movement."[11] From within the flow, differentiations emerge and are for a while distinct before dissolving back into the flow to eventually emerge again in distinctly new configurations. So much are we one that the elements of which we are made were present at the beginning of time. So much are we one that the sound of the beginning is the sound at the heart of the flow now.

Irenaeus, a second-century teacher from the Celtic territory of ancient Gaul, taught that the whole of creation flows forth from the very "substance" of God.[12] All things carry within them the essence of the One. Irenaeus prophetically anticipated the direction of Western Christian thought in the following centuries when he signaled his concern about the doctrine of creation *ex nihilo*, creation out of nothing. By the fourth century this was to become imperial orthodoxy. This was to become the standard of Western Christianity's approach to creation. Creation would be viewed not as coming forth from the substance of God but as fashioned from afar by a distant Creator, made out of nothing from on high.

Irenaeus intuited that this would be a disaster, that to neutralize matter, to teach that creation does not come from holy substance, would lead to the abuse of creation. It was a convenient "truth" to empire in the fourth century when the imperial Church formulated its doctrine of creation *ex nihilo*. It meant that the empire could do whatever it wished to matter. Matter was not holy. It had not come forth from the womb of God's Being. Rather it was made from nothing. It was essentially devoid of sacred energy. So the empire could ravage earth's resources with impunity. It could disparage the rights of creatures and subordinate the physical well-being of its subjects. Religion had become the accomplice of the state's subordination of the earth. It had sanctioned the separation of spirit and matter.

Irenaeus saw some of this coming as early as the second century, when he passionately taught that the substance of the earth and its creatures carries within itself the life of the Holy One. God, he said, is both "above us all and in us all."[13] God is both transcendent and immanent. And the work of Jesus, he taught, was not to save us from our nature but to restore us to our nature and to bring us back into relationship with the deepest sound within creation. In his commentary on the Prologue to St. John's Gospel, in which all things are described as spoken into being by God, Irenaeus sees Jesus not as speaking a new word but as uttering again the first word, the sound at the beginning and the heart of life. He describes Jesus as "recapitulating" the original work of the Creator, as articulating again what we have forgotten and what needs to be repeated, the Sound from which all life has come.[14] Jesus re-sounds the beginning. He resounds with what is deepest in the matter of the universe.

I am writing this book in New Harmony, Indiana, a hidden-away treasure at the heart of the United States. As its name would suggest, New Harmony was the site of a utopian experiment in the nineteenth century. In fact there were two experiments—the Harmonists early in the century followed almost immediately by the Owenites. Both were relatively short lived, but New Harmony continued for some time to be a place of vision in which a new harmony for the earth was being sought. That vision has been reborn over the last fifty years under the inspiration of Jane Blaffer Owen. Her charism in this place has been to preside at the marriage of art and spirituality for the birth of a greater harmony in our world.

In the 1950s, Jane Owen met the sculptor Jacques Lipchitz. During the Second World War, Lipchitz was a renowned Jewish artist in Paris. Such was his international reputation that the Allies arranged for his safe escape from France as the Nazis were occupying Paris. In Europe, as nation after nation fell to Hitler's might, Lipchitz had conceived the idea of a peace sculpture for the church in Assy. But his sudden exile from occupied France cut short the project, and for many years the idea lay dormant.

In America, however, Lipchitz met Jane Owen through another European in exile, the great German theologian Paul Tillich. Jane learned of Lipchitz's Assy project and commissioned him to produce three casts. One was given to Assy, as France reconstructed its life after the war. One was presented to Iona in Scotland, as the historic abbey was being rebuilt as part of the recovery of a spirituality of peace for the world. And the third was for New Harmony in the heartland of the United States, Jane Owen's base of vision for a new harmony among nations and peoples.

The Lipchitz statue, called *The Descent of the Spirit*, is of a strong dove with wide-open eyes of awareness, descending on an abstract feminine shape that is opening to give birth to an innocent lamb. On the back of the statue, Lipchitz inscribed in French the words that translate as "Jacob

Lipchitz, Jew, faithful to the religion of his ancestors, has made this virgin for the goodwill of all mankind that the spirit might prevail."

The statue speaks on many levels. On one level, it is the story at the heart of the Christian household, of the Child of Peace conceived by the Spirit in the womb of Mary the Mother. On another level, it speaks of all that is born, of all life conceived by the Spirit in the womb of the universe. The divine feminine, surrounded by the stars of the cosmos, opens to give birth to everything that has being. All life is holy. The Christ story is the universe story. The birth of the divine-human child is a revelation, a lifting of the veil to show us that all life has been conceived by the Spirit in the womb of the universe, that we are all divine-human crea-tures, that everything that has being in the universe carries within itself the sacredness of Spirit.

We have tragically divided the word *matter* from its Latin root, *mater*, which means "mother." All matter—the matter of the stars and planets, the matter of earth and its fecund energies, the matter of our bodies and their deepest yearnings—all things come forth from the Mother. They are all conceptions of Spirit, which is to say that the matter of the universe is holy. In other words, matter matters. As George MacLeod, the founder of the modern-day Iona Community, used to say, "There is no such thing as dead matter."[15] At the heart of the material is the spiritual. The deeper we move in the matter of the universe, the closer we come to Spirit. So what we do to matter matters—whether that be the matter of our bodies and how we handle one another in relationship, whether that be the matter of the earth and how we handle its sacred resources, or whether that be the matter of the body politic and how we handle the sacredness of one another's sovereignty as nations. Lipchitz's *Descent of the Spirit* calls us back to the sacredness of matter, to the holiness of everything that is born of the *Mater*. It calls us back so that "the Spirit might prevail."

Gerard Manley Hopkins, inspired by the Celtic landscape and culture of north Wales, writes in his one of his greatest poems, "God's Grandeur," "There lives the dearest freshness deep down things."[16] It is what Hildegard calls the "greening power" or the "moistness" of the Spirit that is deep in the body of the earth and the human soul.[17] Hopkins invites us to turn our attention to the "inscape" of things, the inner landscape of creation and the human mystery from which the "dearest freshness" can spring again.[18] Yet instead of walking the earth with awareness, with a sensitivity to the Source that is "deep down things," we have dulled our capacity to feel. "Nor can foot feel, being shod," writes Hopkins.[19] We have become heavy footed, covering over and deadening our deepest faculties of perception.

In the story of Moses and the burning bush, in which the Living Presence is revealed in the words "I am who I am" or "I will be what I will be," Moses is told to take off his shoes, for the ground on which he is standing is holy. He is told to uncover the soles of his feet, a place of deep knowing in the human form. Think of walking barefoot in the grass. Think of placing our bare feet into the coolness of a refreshing stream. When we do so, we see in a new way. Doors of perception are opened in us. Rabbi Nahum, in teaching on this passage from the Torah, likes to say that the important aspect of this story is not that the bush is burning but that Moses notices. For every bush is burning. Every bush is aflame with the Living Presence. The "fiery power," as Hildegard puts it, is hidden in everything that has being.[20]

During my first visit to India, at the ashram of Bede Griffiths in Tamil Nadu, I was struck by the number of times we were barefooted each day. In fact, we were more often barefooted than sandaled. As we greeted the rising sun in meditation on the banks of the River Cauvery in the early dawn. As we prayed and celebrated communion in the chapel that opens immediately onto creation. As we studied sacred texts together in simple thatched huts. As we shared food seated on the tiled floor of the dining hall. As we sang our closing chants at nightfall and walked together in the cool of the evening breeze along the river path. In all of this we were barefooted.

Jung says, "When you walk with naked feet, how can you ever forget the earth?"[21] My transition to the streets of Madras upon leaving the ashram felt harsh. I was not walking with uncovered feet anymore, and I was forgetting the earth. I was forgetting the "deep down things" of the Spirit in matter. On my final evening in the city, as I walked along a simple unlit path leading back to my accommodation, I stumbled over an object on the pathway. It was dark, and I could not see clearly. But when I looked more closely, I saw that it was not just an object on the pathway. It was a little old woman. She was curled up for the night, covered in little more than a sackcloth.

I am ashamed to say that my first thought after stumbling over her was, "I'm glad I wasn't barefooted." Something shameful in me did not want to touch the horrendous wrong of that little woman having to sleep on a pathway. Something in me knew that if I allowed myself to be touched by the disgraceful injustice of her and countless others in our world having to sleep rough every night, I would never be the same. I would have to change. I would have to do something about it.

I left India the next day, changed. My first night's dream had warned me of an anxiety in my heart about this strange land that I was entering. I did not know then what I knew as I left, that we and all things are inextricably linked, that I will not be well as long as a little old woman is sleeping rough on a path, that the Transcendent One is the Immanent One, that I will not be one with God as long as I recoil from touching the suffering of the earth. A *perestroika* of soul was unfolding in me. I was being reconstructed by a dialogue with India. And I knew that I needed to do something about it.

CHAPTER 2

OUTBURSTS OF SINGULARITY

I n the initial months after my first visit to India, there was a particular moment from my Eastern journey about which I was unable to speak without weeping. So for some time I shared it only with a few. But I have come to believe that we need to find ways of sharing our intimate experiences of the Mystery, for we are one. It is through one another that we will know more of the Life that flows within us all. It is through sharing our fragments of insight that we will come to a fuller picture of the One who is at the heart of each life.

Harry Underhill and I had made our way from Madras by train, traveling further south in Tamil Nadu. We arrived at dusk in a little town close to Shantivanam, the monastic community of Bede Griffiths. Our final approach to the ashram was under the cover of night. The bicycle rickshaws in which we were now traveling took us along unlit country paths. Here and there we passed simple peasant dwellings where families gathered in conversation around low evening fires. The scent of dung-fire smoke and a mixture of India's spices wafted in the dark.

I felt as if I was entering an ancient world. Aspects of it were strange to me. I had never been surrounded by such primitive simplicity. Yet it was somehow familiar. It was stirring a recollection deep in my psyche, the forgotten memory of those who have gone before us on earth's journey, the countless generations of mothers and fathers whose life we carry within the psychic layers of our minds and bodies. Edwin Muir, the Scottish poet, says, "The night, the night alone is old and showed me what I knew . . . yet never had been told."[1] I was entering an ancient nighttime, and it held unconscious memory for me. We arrived at Shantivanam as night prayer dispersed. Under the crescent new moon there was just enough light in the sky to see our way along the sandy path that led to the guest master's hut. Brother Martin welcomed us and showed us to our cell for the night.

I woke to the sound of a bell, then soft footsteps padding toward the river for morning meditation. I followed the sound, in the early dawn able to see only the faintest of outlines, and found myself on the banks of the River Cauvery. Others were there, although how many I could not yet tell. They were only shapes, some sitting cross-legged on the ground or with backs against trees, others standing still and attentive, all waiting in silence for the sun's new light. Gradually it came, at first only a faint glow, but then a great brilliance breaking from the east. And in the light of day I was able to see who was there—faces from East and West, men and women from different nations, monks in saffron-colored garments and villagers squatting close to the ground with arms folded on their knees, watching as they have done

since before the dawn of history the coming of a new day.
It seemed deeply familiar to me, even though never in my
life had I meditated at the rising of the sun. It seemed
natural, even though so much of our Western world has
forgotten the practice.

We walked in silence to the chapel for the morning
celebration of mass. The chanting was Eastern; the readings
were Hindu, Christian, Jewish, and Muslim; the offering of
elements included bread and wine, flowers and light; and
the chapel opened without windows on to the sounds
and colors of creation all around us. The symbol of the
third eye and inner wisdom, the red dot or bindi of Hindu
practice, was placed at the center of our foreheads. To grow
in Christ was to grow in wisdom. To be nourished in the
way of Jesus was to be nourished in an ancient way of
seeing that is deep in the human soul, an inner truth
that is not the preserve of one tradition over against another
but a wisdom that precedes and is deeper than our
divisions.

After mass, we washed our hands at the entrance to the
refectory and sat barefooted in two long lines on the floor,
with simple tin plates and cups in front of us. A great pot
of rice and one of curry were brought along each line and
scooped onto our plates, then a ladle each of warm milk
into our cups. We ate in silence using only our hands. I
noticed, as I looked about me taking in this strange new
world, that whereas my right hand was covered in curry
juices all the way up my wrist, the Indian brothers delicately
cupped the food in their fingers and effortlessly into their
mouths without a trace of mess. And adeptly they were well

into their second platefuls long before I had made any impression on my first!

During breakfast, as I looked around the room, I had hoped to spot Bede Griffiths. He was the abbot of Shantivanam, or "Forest of Peace." In his early eighties, he was the guru, the visionary teacher at the heart of this community, who over many decades had shaped a marriage between East and West. Forty years earlier, he had come to India as an English Benedictine monk steeped in the poetry and learning of the West. But the Christ of India, he had come to realize, needed to be stripped of Western clothing so as to be garbed in the wisdom and meditative practices of the East. On my flight to India, I had read his *Return to the Center*, in which he describes God as the Presence at the heart of all life. Our journey toward wholeness, he taught, is not a movement away from what is deepest in us. It is not a looking beyond the matter of creation. Rather, it is a return to God by returning to our true center and to the true center of everything that has being.

After breakfast, I was told that Bede was not well. Only days before my arrival, he had suffered a massive stroke. To begin with it had paralyzed him. Only now was he beginning to recover speech, slowly and falteringly. I asked if I might see him and was told to visit his hut and inquire with the sister who was caring for him. She kindly heard my request and, although protective of Bede, went in immediately to see if he would receive this visitor from Scotland. She then opened the door and motioned me in. Bede was sitting upright in his bed. The window shutters were wide open, and the morning sun dappled through the surrounding trees to fill his room with light. He looked like Moses having just come down from Mount Sinai—white hair, white beard, and radiant countenance.

He wore nothing but an orange dhoti round his waist. His top was bare, and he looked the epitome of an Indian sannyasi, although he greeted me with the accent of an Edwardian gentleman. He invited me to sit down close to his bed. I was a young man. This was entirely new territory to me. Looking back on it now, I realize I had no idea what to say. I lacked the tools even to ask a basic question about this new but ancient realm of prayerful meditation that I had just entered. So instead I stupidly began to talk about Iona. Here I was in the presence of one of the world's greatest Christian teachers. Here I had an opportunity to ask about things I did not yet know, and instead I chose to speak only about what I knew. Bede listened with great interest, asking many, many questions, and then our time was up. And I left his hut not knowing one thing more than when I had entered.

I had not asked a question, so I left without answers. But I did leave with a clear sense that Bede was an extraordinary presence. His face literally shone. His body was frail, but his eyes were bright. And he gave me total attention. It was not until much later that I learned what had happened at the time of his so-called stroke. He had been meditating, and halfway through his prayerful silence he experienced God as feminine. For years, even for decades, he had been teaching the marriage of East and West, the need to hold together the sacred feminine and the sacred masculine. But that was in the realm of thought and idea. This was different. This was a direct experience of the Sacred Feminine. And as he later said, it was too much for his old Western body! It shook him down to the foundations of his being. Medically, it was described as a stroke. Spiritually, it was a moment of illumination.

I spent the rest of the morning sitting on the porch of the ashram library, reading a Western text. I was unaware of it at the time, but clearly I was struggling to integrate my experience of the East. So on my first morning at Shantivanam, I sat reading a Western theologian whom I could just as easily have read in New College Library back in Edinburgh! Before I knew it, the morning was over. My Western mind had been refortified, and I was ready for lunch. Again we sat on the floor of the refectory in long lines to receive curry and rice and yogurt. This time a reading accompanied our silent meal. It was from Bede's most recent publication, *A New Vision of Reality*, in which he traces the convergence between new science and ancient wisdom and speaks of the gift of the East to the emerging science of the West in its unitary vision of reality.

After lunch, in the heat of the early afternoon, we retreated to our cells for siesta. I lay down under my mosquito netting and entered a deep sleep. But I awoke to the briefest of dreams. In the dream, an unknown beautiful young Indian woman came to me and sat on the edge of my bed. Dressed in a richly dark-colored sari, she leaned over me and, looking directly into my eyes, said, "My mother tells me that I have always loved you." I woke up amidst a flood of tears.

For twenty years now, this simple dream has been close to my heart. It was a message from the unconscious. And it was speaking to me, as dreams often do, of what I needed to know, of what I was not yet conscious of in my life. Twenty years later, when I see my daughter Kirsten dressed in a dance sari approaching me at Kalakshetra in Chennai, I often remember the beautiful young woman who came to me in my dream. And perhaps Kirsten is now that messenger from the East in my life, or perhaps it will be Kirsten's daughter in years to come. But at the time, the dream was specifically speaking about something I did not know. What was it?

"My mother tells me that I have always loved you." Part of me did not know that I was loved. Even though I have been so blessed in my life by family love and friends, part of me still did not know. And part of me had lost contact with the Mother, the Mater, the One from whom I am born. Even though I was busy in my life trying to serve the One, trying to play my part in creating a more just world, part of me had lost contact. And part of me had never known that the Mater has as many messengers as there are people in the world. Even though I had been blessed in my religious inheritance to have teachings and symbols that communicated love, I had not even begun to imagine that the East and the realm of the unconscious were also part of my inheritance. The beautiful young woman was Indian. She, like the East, was an unknown messenger to me. And she carried, not what I already knew, but what I still needed to know.

What is it we need to know in our lives? That we are loved. That we have always been loved. We may know that family and friends love us—a gift beyond price. Do we know too that that love issues up from a deeper Source, without beginning and without end, and that it is our only sure hope at moments of failure and crisis in life? We may believe that there is a *Mater* or Living Matrix from which the universe has come and that we should live justly and peacefully together on earth. Do we know too that the birthing presence at the heart of the universe is love? That the universe in its oneness is radically relational? And that it is not just a matter of knowing a law of unity but a Presence of Unity? We may know that we have been blessed in our nations and religions by prophets of wisdom and messengers of truth. Do we also know that every people and every spiritual tradition has been blessed with Sophia and with unique manifestations of the Spirit, and that we will be truly well not in isolation from one another but in relationship? And in all of this again and again and again, do we know that we are loved?

In this ancient world of India, I was beginning to remember. I was beginning to recollect what I had long ago forgotten or perhaps never really known. The dream had opened me to the East. I would not be reading any more Western texts during my mornings at the ashram. There would be time enough for that upon my return home. My days would now be spent drinking at a new well, the ancient well of Eastern thought and meditative practice. The dream had opened me to the East because it had opened me in a new way to Love. Part of my fear of the East had been an anxiety that individuality would be lost in a vision of oneness. The opposite had occurred.

It was through a messenger from the East that I heard a deeply personal word. Teilhard de Chardin, the French priest and scientist who was profoundly affected by his many years in the East, describes it in his autobiographical account as a movement from seeing the "Crimson of Matter," in which everything shone with sacredness, to the "Incandescence of Some One," in which he recognized a Living Presence at the heart of matter.[2] My time in India had opened me in a new way to the "Incandescence of Some One," to the Some One within the unconscious, to the Some One who was clothed in the East, to the Some One at the heart of life.

I draw from dreams because they have been important in my life and journey. But I draw from my dreams also because I believe they issue up from a place within us, not simply from within me. They are a way of accessing our depths, not simply my depths. Jung speaks of this shared wellspring within the human mystery as the collective unconscious, that unknown realm from which our lives and all life emerge. Dreams, he says, are "saying things beyond our conscious comprehension."[3] In dreams, the unconscious, which is shared and deep within us all, is trying to enter consciousness through the particularity of our individual lives. A dream will often speak of what is common to us all, even though it comes through the radical uniqueness of our own individual experiences and dream life.

Robert Johnson, a psychotherapist in the Jungian tradition, says that dreams are "the speech of God."[4] That is not to say that we do not need to argue with them. Arguing or

wrestling with dreams, as Jacob did with the angel who
visited him in the night, is part of the revelatory process. It
is as essential in dreams as it is in any other channel of
revelation, whether that be "the speech of God" in Scripture
or in creation. In all these realms, there is much that can
seem like nonsense or much that can appear antithetical
to the sacred. So in any discipline of revelation, we need to
wrestle our way toward clarity rather than simply accept
passively what we have received. And we do this not merely
on our own but together. It is in the most significant
relationships of our lives and in communion with the
people and inherited treasure of our wisdom traditions that
we are called to wrestle our way together toward greater
consciousness.

Jung says that our "worst sin is unconsciousness."[5] To
live unaware either of the glory that is within us or the
shadow that is within us is to be prone to falseness. And to
be unconscious either of the oneness of life or the radical
individuality of everything that has being is to fall out of
relationship with the wholeness of which we are a part.
During our wakeful hours, in the light of day, we tend to
see the differentiation of the parts. We tend to see how one
person or one creature is distinct from another. At night, in
contrast, in our dreams just as in meditative practice, we are
reminded of the oneness and the interwovenness of all
things. Dreams, says Jung, rise from "all-uniting depths"
within us.[6] In our dreams, one person will suddenly become
another person, or one place will unexpectedly merge
into another place. Fixed boundaries are dissolved. Shape-
shifting and the metamorphic become the norm. In dreams

we are being invited to remember the one river that flows through life's boundless multiplicities.

But we need both ways of seeing if we are to be whole. We need dreamlike consciousness to remember life's oneness. And we need midday consciousness to cherish the uniqueness of each part. It is a two-eyed consciousness that we are needing to recover if we are to live in a balance between life's essential unity and life's radical individualities. Jung speaks of the "Sol" (the sun) being our right eye, and the "Luna" (the moon) being our left.[7] Sun-like consciousness and moon-like consciousness converge to form a whole.

In the mid-1990s, I was an assistant minister at St. Giles in Edinburgh. It is a national cathedral in which affairs of the nation are marked and in which people from around the world pray every day alongside men and women of Scotland. I arrived at the cathedral in a depleted state, exhausted from the exhilarating demands and tensions of four years of leadership at the abbey on Iona. Much of me felt a failure. I had not managed to live the integration and balance of personal life and community life, of prayer and commitment, of inner awareness and outward action that I had been awakened to in India. But the cathedral welcomed me. I had been a student in Edinburgh in the 1970s, and it received me back like a son. I needed its sanctuary and was grateful.

Early in my time at St. Giles, I had a dream. In the dream, I had only one functioning eye. My second eye was grown over by skin and a grotesque covering of hair. It was a disturbing dream. I did not yet have many tools for interpreting the unconscious, but it was at least clear to me that I was being invited to recover a way of seeing that had been lost or covered over in my life. And, although I did not recognize the significance at the time, the eye that was covered over was my left eye, my Luna eye. I see now that the dream was inviting me to recover a more unitary vision of life, that what I needed was to regain a sense of the whole. And only then would I be able to see the parts more clearly. Only then would I be able to see my part more clearly—what my own path and my own individuality should be.

Jung says that the ego is the "*sina qua non* of consciousness."[8] We will be truly well only to the extent that we are aware of life's oneness. But we will be aware of life's oneness only to the extent that our ego is developed. At birth, our ego has not yet formed, so everything is experienced as a sea of undifferentiated oneness. Only gradually do we become aware of life's differentiations. And it is the development of the ego that enables us to do that. Part of what we deeply owe our children and one another is the fostering of a strong sense of selfhood that can distinguish between the one and the many, the parts and the whole. The ego must first learn to distinguish before it can then reunite.

The problem for many of us, however, and the problem that faces many of our religious traditions and cultural norms, is that the development of our consciousness has been arrested. It has stopped short. We have learned to distinguish between the parts, between individuals and nations and species, but we have failed to go on to reunite them.

We have graduated from undifferentiated oneness, but have neglected to move on to differentiated oneness. And the result is that our individuality has been undermined because we have forgotten what it truly rests on, our oneness. Consequently the ego, whether the ego of the human species or the ego of our nation or the ego of our religious tradition, has asserted itself falsely as the center of life rather than as the faculty that exists to serve our consciousness of the whole. We will be well to the extent that we live in relationship with one another, in relationship to the whole, rather than serving the limited egos of our lives and nations and species.

The St. Giles dream in which my left eye was covered with skin and hair was speaking to me of a half-consciousness. It was speaking of a way of seeing in which individuality, whether my individuality or the individuality of others and of other nations, was viewed with only one eye. I was losing my way in life because I was forgetting the whole. And in forgetting the whole it was impossible to remember the true glory of the parts. It is only when we see the oneness of life that the true beauty of our differentiations comes into full view. The new Pentecost in which we are living, the new awareness of life's essential oneness, is freeing us to move from half-consciousness into a consciousness of the whole. And when we see the whole, we will, as Rabbi Abraham Heschel says, be able to truly celebrate life's "outbursts of singularity."[9] Rather than feeling threatened by differentiation, we will see it as an intrinsic part of wholeness. Rather than separating so-called opposites, we will welcome them as completing each other.

In the East, which is characterized by a sense of life's unity, I had received a personal message of love. In the West, in contrast, with its passionate advocacy of individuality, I had received a dream that prompted me to reclaim a vision of life's oneness. Whether in the East or the West, we are being invited to recover this balance. And whether in the East or the West, for the world's well-being and for our own individual well-being, we need to know that all things are interwoven and that each strand in the tapestry is holy. We need to know that our distinct races, our countless species, our many wisdom traditions, our children, and the men and women of every nation are wonderful "outbursts of singularity," each carrying within them the life of the One.

Here in New Harmony, one of my favorite places of prayer is the sculpture by Tobi Kahn, a renowned Jewish artist from New York. The piece is called *Shalev*, or *Angel of Compassion*. It is a twelve-foot-high granite archway under which the angel of compassion is passing. She is a life-sized human figure made of gleaming bronze, and her head and entire posture incline with presence. The archway has always felt to me like the archway of the present moment, the archway of every moment. And the angel is like a messenger of the Living Presence, inclining with compassion, accompanying us and our world as we enter the archway of the present. Beside the sculpture is a plaque inscribed with words from a Jewish mystic. It reads, "Each Human Being is a partner of the Blessed Holy One."

A number of years ago during one of my visits to New Harmony, I was walking along the Wabash River, which flows with its broad and mighty current along the outskirts of town. It was evening, and halfway through my walk a wild storm blew in. I was close to the *Angel of Compassion*, and there was no other place to seek shelter. I felt awkward about physically entering a piece of art, but, believing that my brother Tobi Kahn would forgive me, I huddled under the great granite archway and found myself standing immediately next to the angel of compassion.

It was dark, and I could not remember exactly what the sculpture's words of inscription were, but my memory was, "Every Human Being is the Beloved of the Nameless Eternal One." So, as the wind and rain whirled about me in the darkness and the sound of the river in spate grew, I began to repeat over and over a simple prayer in my heart. "May I know that I am beloved. May I know that I am beloved. May I know that I am beloved." My mind took me to haunted places within myself where I doubt that I am beloved—places in my body and mind and soul. I remembered times in my life when I had been ugly and false in my actions. I thought of how little I was doing for the transformation of the world, of how little of myself I was giving away for the sake of others. "May I know that I am beloved," I prayed. "May I know that I am beloved."

After a while, the storm abated. It was time to leave and head back to town. Or so I thought. I was only fifty yards from the archway when the rains came again. They drove me back to the angel of compassion for a second time. So again I prayed, but this time the words were, "May she know that she is beloved. May she know that she is beloved." I named within myself people whom I love. I thought of my sister who had experienced betrayal and the collapse of her

marriage. I longed for her to know that she was beautiful
in her mind and body and soul. That she was beloved. I
thought of my friend struggling through chemotherapy and
seeking the strength to look death in the face. "May he know
that he is beloved. May he know that he is beloved."

Again the storm dropped. And again I began to walk
toward town, but a third time the rains came and drove me
back to the angel. So for a third time I prayed. But this time
it was, "May we know that we are beloved. May we know
that we are beloved." My thoughts turned to Iraq, to
Palestine, to places of deep wrong and abuse in our cities
and among us as nations, where we forget that the other is
beloved. My heart was aware of children who doubt that
they are loved because of the neglect they suffer. I thought
of creatures and entire species who are struggling because
of our failure to love the earth. "May we know that we are
beloved. May we know that we are beloved."

Is there a prayer more central than this? Is there something deeper than this for us to know in our bodies and
minds if we are to be well and if we are to give ourselves
for one another's well-being? Three times I was led to the
angel. Three times I prayed these words in repetition. But I
suppose it is three times a day that I need to pray them, or
three times an hour. I know that I need this prayer, and I
know that my journey is only one particular expression of
the common journey of humanity and the earth. I know
that my need is part of our need and part of the earth's need.
And I know that I not only need the angel of compassion
in the archway of this moment in my life but that I am part
of the messenger of compassion in the archway of this

moment in our world. If together we are to be well, we must know ourselves to be bearers of compassion, inclining to one another and to the earth with presence.

Tobi Kahn's uncle, Arthur Kahn, was among the first deportation of Jews to Dachau in Nazi Europe. There, as a young man, he was executed by a German firing squad. Part of Tobi Kahn's greatness as an artist is that, despite the deep wrong that his family and people endured during the war, he sees compassion, not hatred, as the way forward. Compassion is the only way forward if we are to be well. Compassion for those who do not know that they are beloved. Compassion for the children and creatures who are suffering today. Compassion even for the people and the nations who wrong us. Revenge has no future, apart from bitterness and the multiplication of wrong. As Mahatma Gandhi taught his people in the midst of his nation's struggle for justice and liberation, the philosophy of revenge, of an eye for an eye, will only make the whole world blind. If what we are committed to is transformation, then the only way forward is compassion, not revenge. A passion that is with and for the other as well as oneself, a passion that is with and for the other *as* oneself.

In the Christian household, we hear the story of Jesus' baptism in the River Jordan. As he emerges from the water, the words from heaven are heard: "This is my Beloved Son with whom I am well pleased" (Matthew 3:17). Jesus, the beloved one, the one who shows us not a foreign truth but the deepest truth—that each one of us is beloved, that each species is cherished, that each nation and each race is holy. These are words that apply not exclusively to Jesus, but to

Jesus as the revelation, the one who lifts the veil to show us who we are, the beloved of God.

In the Nicene Creed that is repeated week after week by Christians around the world, Jesus is referred to as "the only Son of God, eternally begotten of the Father." This has come to be understood, and perhaps in the fourth-century imperial church was intended to be understood, as exclusively referring to Jesus. Over the centuries it has been used to give the impression that Jesus is of God in a way that does not apply to the rest of creation. Jesus comes out of the very substance of the Holy, but the rest of creation is fashioned from afar by a distant Creator.

The fourteenth-century mystic Meister Eckhart offers us another way of seeing. In his commentary on St. John's Gospel, where the phrase "only-begotten" is used, Eckhart explains that it means "born from the One."[10] Jesus is begotten from the Only One. In that sense he is Only-begotten. He reveals not an exclusive truth that applies limitedly to him. He reveals the most inclusive of truths, that all things are of the One, that everything issues from the Womb at the heart of the cosmos. The whole universe is Only-begotten. And not only is the whole universe holy, but each part of the universe is holy. Each part of the whole is Only-begotten.

The twelfth-century teacher Hildegard of Bingen, in one of her dreamlike visions, hears the words of assurance, "You were planted in my heart at daybreak on the first day of creation."[11] These words speak of the precious individuality of Hildegard, of the uniqueness of her body and mind and soul, of the singularity of her utterances and her creativities. They speak also of the cherished individuality of each created thing, of the sacred uniqueness of our bodies and our minds and our souls, of the holy singularity of every strand of existence in the cosmos. Each one of us appeared in the heart of God at daybreak on the first day.

My Shantivanam dream was with me as I left the ashram. The words of the beautiful young Indian woman still sounded in my heart, "My mother tells me that I have always loved you." In the early morning of my departure, Harry Underhill walked with me to the nearest roadway. We said our farewells in the dark as I climbed onto a crowded bus that would take me to Trichy and from there by train to Madras. The smell of India, the breakfast fires on the side of the road along our route, the honking of horns at every turn and every passing vehicle, the relative coolness of the early morning air breezing through the bus's open windows—all merged within me in a single sense of gratitude for India. In the dark of predawn on the bus, I was not yet able to make out the distinct faces of my fellow passengers. The outlines of shapes were of old men, young children, mothers feeding, but in the dark there was no definition of faces, only a common journey.

Dawn was breaking by the time we reached the Trichy train station. We found it surrounded by military. Armed guards stood with Kalashnikov rifles. All passengers were required to show identification and travel tickets before being allowed through the cordon. The previous night there had been political unrest along the line. A train had been overturned by angry antigovernment protesters. We were pointed to train cars with metal shutters pulled down and locked tight on the outside. We set off from Trichy in our closed-in compartments, and within a few hundred yards began to hear the shouts of protesters and rocks hurled at the train.

For the next two hours it was the same at every station— the sound of angry shouting and the crash of hard objects and sticks clattering against the metal shutters. The calm of the ashram was behind me. I had not forgotten the promise of my dream, but I was hearing it now amid the struggle of a nation. "My mother tells me that I have always loved you." These words are spoken for each of us. And I was listening now for what they meant in the lives of those on the other side of the shutters—even amid their anger—in the families of the men and women shouting for better work conditions and better pay. I was listening to determined outbursts of singularity.

There is a unity in the human soul and deep within the body of the universe. Each created thing, each human being carries the sound of the Only One. We will truly hear it only when we pay attention to the singularity of each note, to the plight of each species, to the hope of each nation, to the longing of each family, each one Only-begotten.

CHAPTER 3

KEEP ON
REMEMBERING

B ede Griffiths died in 1994. A few weeks after his
death, he appeared to me in a dream. He said, "Keep
on reading 'Sleeping Beauty.' Keep on reading
'Sleeping Beauty.'" That was it. Nothing else. Just the words,
"Keep on reading 'Sleeping Beauty.'" The dream was speaking of something that had fallen asleep in me, a beauty
within us, within our depths that is waiting to be
reawakened. It was speaking not of a beauty that has died
or been extinguished but of a beauty that is paralyzed or
forgotten.

In Grimm's fairy tale "Sleeping Beauty," what is it that
happens to the beautiful princess to put her into a sleep
that is almost like death, a paralysis so deep that it affects
her entire household for a hundred years? The princess had
been a child of promise, born of the barren king and queen,
begotten as if by magic. So grateful was the king for her
birth that he prepared a splendid feast to which the whole
kingdom was invited, including the fairies of the land. There
were thirteen fairies in all, but the king had only twelve
golden plates for them. One of the fairies had to be excluded,

so it was the spiteful old fairy who was not included on the guest list.

At the party, gifts were presented to the child. The good fairies took it in turn to bless her with beauty and riches and kindness. But just before the twelfth fairy offered her blessing, the mean old fairy appeared and cursed the child. In her fifteenth year, said the fairy, the princess would prick herself with a spindle and die. Amidst the horror of this pronouncement, the twelfth fairy, who had not yet offered her blessing, stepped forward and spoke. She could not undo the curse of the unkind fairy, but she could redeem it with a final blessing. The child, she said, would not die. Rather she would fall into a deep sleep for one hundred years.

Fifteen years later, the princess did prick her finger. Although the king in fear had banned all spinning wheels from the kingdom, there was one old spinning woman who was so deaf that she had not heard the king's order. Early on the morning of her fifteenth birthday, the princess wandered into a neglected tower room in the castle, and there was the old woman spinning. The princess, having never been told about the curse, was intrigued by the whirling sound of the wheel and asked to have a turn. No sooner had she started at the wheel than she pricked her finger. The sleep that immediately fell upon her was so deep that it took the whole household with her, and they slept for one hundred years.

"Keep on reading 'Sleeping Beauty,'" said Bede in my dream. "Keep on reading 'Sleeping Beauty.'" Why did the princess fall into a deathlike sleep? What might have prevented it? If the mean fairy had been included in the feast rather than shunned, perhaps she would not have cursed the princess. Or if the king had not reacted in such fear to the malicious curse, perhaps his daughter could have been made conscious of the risk instead of kept innocent to the danger. Or if the old spinning woman had not been so deaf, perhaps there would have been no occasion for the princess to prick her finger.

There are many ifs in this story, just as there are many ifs in our lives as to why we forget what is truly within us or why the beauty of our nature has become paralyzed. In Grimm's fairy tale, they all relate, in one way or another, to awareness and fear and themes of wholeness. If my dream was speaking about some aspect of beauty that India had given me but that needed to be further awakened, how were my awareness and my fear and my sense of wholeness contributing?

Bede represented for me someone who had integrated the East and the West, the masculine and the feminine, Spirit and matter, the night and the day, the conscious and the unconscious, the head and the heart, the one and the many. And one of the most practical gifts that he represented for me and that I had received during my time at the ashram was a form of meditation. It was a simple method for accessing awareness of the Divine, for waking up to the sleeping beauty of our true depths.

On one of my first evenings at Shantivanam, I walked along the River Cauvery with a kind old monk. We spoke about meditation and about an ancient form of prayer that was used by many of the brothers at the ashram. It derived from the East. I was a novice in this realm. I knew virtually nothing about meditative prayer. As a Church of Scotland minister, I had been trained neither in the way of prayer nor in the practice of meditation. The focus had been on pure theology, with fragments of instruction on preaching and pastoral work. This continues to be a gap in most seminaries in the Western world today, a tragic void of instructive practice about silence and prayer.

I asked the old Indian monk to teach me the way of meditation. I had noticed it being practiced in the life of the ashram, but did not know how to access it. During the silences in prayer and during morning meditation, my mind was easily distracted, skipping from one thought to another. As it is said in the East, the human mind is like a tree with thousands of monkeys in it swinging continuously from one branch to another. This was my experience in silent meditation. I sensed that there must be more to it than this.

The old monk spoke to me of one of the most ancient forms of meditation that has been practiced in the Hindu world and has been baptized into the Christian tradition in places like Shantivanam over the centuries. It is both ancient and simple, which is not to say that it is easy. Monkeys will always continue to swing in the mind. But the method itself is simple when the will is focused. It consists of a silent repetition of the word "Om" in time with one's breath. During inhalation, the word "Om" is silently intoned. This is then repeated during exhalation. In the intake of breath, Oooommmm. In the outward flow of breath, Oooommmm. In and out, a steady silent intonation of the word that in Hinduism means the First Word. It is the name of the Self within all selves. It is the sound of the One at the beginning from whom the life of the universe and all life comes.

It seemed so simple when the old Shantivanam monk explained this to me. And I was so ready to learn. My heart had been opened to the East. I was eager to try. Even as I went off to sleep that night, I was practicing Oooommmm, Oooommmm as I breathed in and out. But it was not until the next morning that I had my first true experience of meditative discipline. Down by the River Cauvery I sat with my back pressed against a tree for support, and in the darkness of the predawn waited with others for the coming light. I silently intoned the First Word, allowing my breath to set the pace. Oooommmm, as I breathed in. Oooommmm, as I breathed out. And soon I became aware of the Sound of the Beginning as something that sounded also within me. It was a simple and real experience of oneness.

I was fortunate to have such a focused time of meditation that morning. Often that is not the case for me. Often I struggle with distractions during meditative prayer. But on that occasion I was very present. It of course had something to do with the context and the other people meditating. This is often the case in my experience. To meditate prayerfully with others can be qualitatively different from meditating on one's own. Both are essential to the discipline of meditation, but to meditate with others can be to find a greater strength and focus. And it can lead to a deeper and more sustained experience of Presence.

I now began to meditate every day at the ashram, in the morning and evening times of meditation, following the ancient practice of prayer at the rising and the setting of the sun. But I would also meditate on my own at different points in the day, sometimes down by the river halfway through the afternoon, sometimes seated on the porch of the library halfway through reading a book, and sometimes even halfway through a sermon at morning mass.

And what I noticed in this newfound practice that I now slipped into and out of so easily was that my meditation experiences of Presence were not different from my non-meditation experiences of Presence. The peace that I experienced during meditation was the same as the peace that I had sometimes experienced as a little boy lying in the grass staring up into the open skies. The oneness that I experienced during meditation was the same as the oneness that I had sometimes experienced lying on my bed at home entering the half-consciousness of sleep. The difference was that in meditative practice, I was intentionally making myself available to an experience of peace. I was consciously choosing to wake up, to further open the doors of perception within myself to the beauty of the One.

Over the years, I have continued this practice, although I have found it helpful to root it more specifically in our Western inheritance. Instead of Om, for instance, I will sometimes use the words *Alpha* and *Omega* as I breathe in and out, allowing myself to be aware of the Beginning and the End, the One who is our source and our destiny. Or at other times I will use a phrase of Scripture—"With my whole heart I seek you" (Psalm 119:10), for instance, or "Do not let your heart be troubled" (John 14:27)—during my outward flow of breath, and then in silence breathe in an awareness of God.

During my doctoral studies at the University of Edinburgh in the late 1970s, I had been helped to see the relationship between the holy and the ordinary. My PhD thesis was on the life and teachings of a so-called heretic in nineteenth-century Scotland, Alexander John Scott. As a young minister in the Church of Scotland he had been deposed from the ministry on a charge of heresy for refusing to sign the Church's Westminster Confession of Faith, in which God's love is limited to the elect. Scott taught not only that the divine love is for everything that has been created but that the Living Presence is within everything that has been created. In Scott I found language for my experience as a boy lying in the grass gazing up into the infinity of the heavens. I found a way of integrating a love of the natural with a love of the holy. And it was in Scott that I first heard that there is a sacred harmony deep within all things. So I began to relate my deepest religious experiences with my deepest natural experiences. This is what I observed too at Shantivanam. The glimpses into Presence that came through meditation were the same as the glimpses into Presence that came through creation. The difference was that meditation was offering me a discipline of awareness, a simple method of prayerfully awakening to what we are often asleep to.

It was also Alexander Scott who taught me that our deepest desire is for union, for a oneness with what is deepest in creation and what is deepest in one another. And in and through all of this was the desire for union with God. Scott did not go on to explicitly state that even our deep sexual desire for union is an expression of our desire for the One. He was too much a nineteenth-century Victorian to make this link explicit. But I as a young man in the twentieth century, newly married, began to realize that my holy desire for union with my wife was part of my desire for union with God. I had known for a long time in our relationship that I longed to be one with her. What I had not known was that this longing was part of the longing to be one with God.

Carl Jung says that sexual union is a genuine "experience of the Divine."[1] It is an experience of the essential harmony at the heart of life. It is a reaching through the physical into the spiritual. It is a dissolving of our separateness back into the oneness from which we have come. I was fortunate to have intuited this through the teachings of Scott, but there was nothing in my religious inheritance to guide me on this path. Our Christian household, unlike most of humanity's other wisdom traditions, has tended to deny the connection between spirituality and sexuality. We have focused instead on the shadow side of sexual desire, naming the self-indulgence and abuse of sexual energy, both of which need to be named if we are to be well within ourselves and in our relationships. But if we fail to first of all name the holiness of sexual desire, and its capacity to further awaken us to the beauty that is at the heart of the other, then we will undermine our attempts at truly safeguarding it.

Meditation is part of our desire for the One. And it can be part of our waking to the beauty of oneness. It is not opposed to holy natural desire. It is a way to discipline holy desire. It is a way of being reminded again and again that

the holy longing for oneness is deep within us and that the
true heart of our longing is desire for God. Meditation is
not opposed to our passion for creation or our passion
for love and the delights of committed sexual relationship.
It is not leading us into a different dimension than the
most blessed natural experiences of oneness. As the twelfth-
century teacher Hildegard of Bingen says, "God has a
burning love for the flesh."[2] And there are four stages, she
says, in the ascent of holy knowing: "seeing, hearing, smell-
ing, and tasting."[3] Our desire is to see and hear oneness in
relationship. Our longing is to smell and taste oneness with
the earth. Meditation is a discipline that serves this desire
and longing. It is a practice that can help us taste oneness.

Teilhard de Chardin in his prayer to matter says, "let
your whole being lead me towards God."[4] We are invited
to leave the surface, he says, and plunge into the divine
milieu "where the soul is most deep and where matter is
most dense."[5] At the heart of matter is the heart of God. At
the center of everything that has being is the center of the
Beautiful One. The great mystery of Christianity, he says, is
not the "appearance" of God in the universe but the "trans-
parence" of God in the universe.[6] The incarnation is not so
much an epiphany, a manifestation of transcendent Presence,
as a diaphany, an opening to disclose the Living Presence at
the heart of all life. In Jesus, he says, we glimpse a synthesis
of what "we could never have dared join together," heaven
and earth, spirit and matter, the divine and the human, the
one and the many.[7]

So what name are we to give to the One who is at the
heart of our being and at the heart of all being? How are

we to utter our awareness of the beauty deep within this moment and every moment, the Om of our beginnings, the Sound from which the universe flows forth? Meister Eckhart, in speaking of the Name that is above every name, says that it is not so much "unnameable" as "omninameable."[8] The name of every creature, every star, every galaxy is the Holy Name. The presence of every person, every parent, every child is the Sacred Presence. The One whose name is beyond definition is the One whose name is each of us, closer than our very breathing.

So how are we to remember? How are we to keep on remembering? The nineteenth-century poet and novelist George MacDonald tells the story of a land that has become barren. Into this wasteland the protagonist of the story wanders. So parched is the land and so weary is the wanderer that he collapses to the ground and falls into a deep sleep. In his sleep he dreams of a river running deep within the earth "playing . . . ethereal harmonies with the stones of their buried channels."[9] It is a subterranean flow far beneath the barren desert. On waking he realizes that he can hear something of that flow deep beneath him. And the more aware he becomes of the subterranean river, the closer it comes to the surface, until finally it bursts forth again, and the land once more becomes green. It is a story that points to the relationship between dream life and awareness, on the one hand, and, on the other, between the awareness of what we have forgotten and transformation in our lives and world.

Kenneth White in his poem "The House of Insight" speaks of "re-membering," of "getting it all together."[10] To remember is to re-member. It is to get back together again what has been separated. Part of what needs to be re-membered within us and between us is the beauty of our oneness. We have lived a dismemberment, a tearing apart of what belongs together, East and West, spirit and matter, the well-being of one nation and the well-being of another, the masculine and the feminine, the one and the many. And as we re-member, writes White, we will recover what he calls "wonderful understanding" or "wunderstanding," a combination of wonder at the whole of reality along with a conscious understanding of each part.[11] Or, as Rabbi Heschel calls it, "radical amazement," which is the true basis for understanding.[12]

A number of years ago, I met a Jewish man from New Jersey. We spoke about most important moments in our lives. He remembered how as a boy growing up in a Hasidic community in New York he used to spend his summers at a camp for Jewish boys just outside the city. On one occasion, word got round that the rebbe, the much-loved rabbi of their community, was downstream from the camp and that he wanted to see the boys. They rushed down the riverside to find the rebbe. And there he was standing in the middle of the stream rocking back and forth, in mantric motion, or in what the Jewish mystics call "one-pointed concentration"—focusing on the heart of the moment as the place where God is to be found, at the heart of every moment.[13]

The boys joined the rebbe in the river. He said only one thing to them. "The water that we see flowing past us now will never flow past us again." He then returned to his rocking movement of prayer. And the boys too began to rock in prayer. But the combination of the flowing water and the rocking movement of prayer put the young boy to sleep. When he woke up, all the other boys were away, but the rebbe was holding him with one arm as he continued to rock in prayer. This time the rabbi did not say anything. He simply looked into the boy's face and smiled. And in the rebbe's face the boy glimpsed the face of the One. The rebbe's countenance was like an icon, a window that opened into the Divine. The young boy, now a middle-aged man, forever held this memory within him. For him it was a way of re-membering.

Max Weber, the social historian, describes the modern world as "disenchanted." Since the Enlightenment, the body of the earth and heaven's body of planets and stars have increasingly been seen as soulless.[14] The sense of the numinous has been withdrawn from matter. And the mind and consciousness have been almost exclusively identified with the human. So the properties that we specifically identify with humanity, such as feeling and thought and soulfulness, have been viewed as incongruent with the rest of the universe. They have been seen as exceptions to the cosmos rather than as emerging from the very heart of the cosmos.

Whenever I arrive at Albuquerque airport in New Mexico, on my way to our little retreat center of Casa del Sol in the high desert, I take a shuttle bus to the car rental depot. At the start of the bus journey, a prerecorded announcement begins, "Welcome to the Land of Enchantment." When I hear these words, I know I have

arrived home in New Mexico. Its pure blue skies, the imme-
diacy of the heavens at night, its great sandstone mesas
magically carved by the elements over millennia, and the
vastness of its desert stretches all form a deeply enchanted
landscape for me. I also know that there is much about New
Mexico that is not enchanted. I know that over the centuries
in this land there has been a tragic displacement and degradation of the native peoples by successive waves of
European immigration and conquest. I know that this land
houses the Los Alamos National Laboratory, where the
atomic bomb that killed more than two hundred thousand
Japanese men and women and children at Hiroshima and
Nagasaki in August 1945 was designed. I know that this is
not straightforwardly a beautiful Land of Enchantment. But
for me and for countless others this is still a deeply spiritual
landscape. It is a place of re-membering.

There are certain places on this planet—for me they
are places like the high desert of New Mexico and Iona
and New Harmony—where we more immediately remember the soul of creation. They are sometimes described as
thin places, translucent landscapes where the division
between spirit and matter can scarcely be discerned. The veil
that divides, says George MacLeod, is "thin as gossamer."[15]
These places are like sacraments. They disclose to us the
thinness that is everywhere present but that we often fail to
access. They shine with a beauty that we often live in forgetfulness of.

Theo Dorgan in his poem "The Promised Garden"
writes, "There is a garden at the heart of things. Our oldest
memory guards it with her strong will."[16] How do we

access that memory? How do we enable one another to remember, to wake up to the harmony that we are bearers of?
The enchantment of such outer landscapes is not unrelated
to the inner landscape of our souls. What is deepest in us
has emerged from the heart of the cosmos. We are not
an exception to the universe. We are a unique expression
of the universe. William Blake, the English poet, speaks of
the universe within that is "starry and glorious."[17] The
inner landscape of our being is as infinite as the outer universe is boundless. And as Thomas Berry says, if we are
"microcosmos," if we carry within us something of the
vastness and the unfolding mystery of the universe, then the
universe is "macroanthropos": the universe carries within
itself something of the intimacy and the longings of the
human soul.[18]

In New Harmony there is the Roofless Church. I can
see its outline from the window of the Poet's House, where
I am writing. The Roofless Church is one of the most prophetic sites of prayer in the Western world. Fifty years ago,
long before the earth consciousness of today, Jane Owen
commissioned the architect Philip Johnston to design a
place of prayer that opened out onto creation. It has four
defining walls but no roof. The Lipchitz statue *The Descent of
the Spirit* stands at the heart of the church, and above the
statue there is a canopy that appears suspended between
heaven and earth, but the church itself has no enclosure. It
is a sanctuary that refuses to separate heaven from earth,
East from West, the gathering place of prayer from the
vastness of the cosmos, the liturgies and celebrations of a
particular people from the rest of humanity. It is a sacred

site that announces that we will be well, not in enclosed separations from one another as nations and wisdom traditions and species, but that we will be well to the extent that we open again to the oneness from which we and all things have come.

Recently when I was praying in the Roofless Church, I met a gardener who was working inside its four walls. He said to me, "I don't often cut grass inside churches." Partly in jest but also in earnest I replied, "The day is coming when there will be grass inside every church." That may not literally prove to be the case. We will probably continue to need spaces in which to gather, in which we are sheltered from the extremes of the elements, places that nurture our togetherness and community. But unless we find ways of opening our sacred sites onto creation, either literally, as in the case of the Roofless Church, or symbolically in terms of pointing again and again to creation as the true cathedral of the Living Presence, then we will be increasingly irrelevant to the new Pentecost. And if we choose to ignore the mighty untamed movement of the Spirit that is inviting us to live not the holiness of separateness but the holiness of wholeness, then our sacred sites will more and more fall into ruin. And on that day grass will grow inside them anyway.

One of my other favorite sites of prayer in the world is the nunnery on Iona in the Hebrides of Scotland. It also is a place without a roof. It also is a place in which people gather to pray because it opens onto the vastness of creation and the oneness of the world. And it also is a place to which people bring the brokenness of their lives and the brokenness of their nations, seeking healing and new beginnings. But the big difference between the nunnery of Iona and the Roofless Church of New Harmony is that the nunnery opens onto creation because of neglect and failure. It is a ruin that came about through abandonment. What we need now, in addition to ruins that open accidentally onto creation, are places of intention and commitment, of new creativity and a new openness to the work of the Spirit in the earth and in the human soul. What we need are places like the Roofless Church, altars of prayer that are built for the oneness of the world.

One of the great features of the early Christian mission in the Celtic world was that it knew very little of worshipping in enclosed spaces. The common practice was to gather around high-standing crosses, some of which at their peak of artistic expression reached twelve feet in height. This was to know the boundlessness of the Spirit. This was to be renewed in the context of earth, sea, and sky. This was to seek renewal in relationship to all things. It was a tragic moment in the history of British Christianity, and consequently for much of the Western world, when in the seventh century, after the Synod of Whitby, the imperial mission forced on the Celtic lands a form of enclosed worship. The architectural norm became the four strong stone walls and the enclosed roof design that we now so much associate with ecclesiastical structure. Thus the impression was created that those who gathered inside the walls were somehow more holy than those who did not, and that the time of gathering and the place of gathering were somehow more sacred than all time and all space.

When I was an assistant minister at St. Giles Cathedral in the early 1990s, I had a dream. In the dream, I was standing in the pulpit preaching. But above me there was no enclosure. It was a roofless cathedral. I did not yet know about the Roofless Church of New Harmony, but it was similar. It opened up into the vastness of the cosmos. But below me, separating me from the congregation, was an artificial ceiling. I was aware that the people could hear me, but I could not see them. So in the dream I had to make a decision. Should I descend from the pulpit and speak under an artificial ceiling, or should I remain in the pulpit and speak from an unenclosed space?

That is a decision that we are being invited to make today in our Christian household and in the various households of our lives and world. Will we continue to speak from enclosed separations—racially, economically, religiously, politically—or will we seek a new open space in which to communicate across the boundaries that have artificially separated us? And will we as a human species continue to pretend that we are in an essentially different category from the rest of creation, or will we seek a new vision, a new-ancient understanding of the one Life that is in every species and in every atom of the universe? In the dream, I chose to remain in the pulpit. I chose the unbounded space into which we are being invited to speak again of oneness.

Recently I dreamed that I was having a telephone conversation with Dipankar, the father of my Indian son-in-law. He said to me, "Is there someone in India with whom you are needing to have a conversation?" In the dream I answered,

"No." To which Dipankar asked, "Are you sure?" "Yes," I answered. But two more times he asked me if I was sure, and two more times I answered in the affirmative. I then asked him how the wound on his head was. He had cut his forehead during the time of our daughter's wedding earlier in the year. The time of the dream was early morning on Easter Sunday. It bore a striking similarity to the Easter story of Jesus asking Simon Peter three times if he loved him.

When I woke up, I was not at all sure that I did not need to have a conversation with India. The dream had been persistent on that front. Three times I was asked the question. And each time I became less sure about my answer. So my waking thoughts took me again to Bede. He represented a lifetime of conversation with India. He lived and loved his dialogue with the East. It was integral to his own journey into wholeness. And it was central to his gift of teaching. The dream confirmed for me what I was already wondering. Should we give more time to conversation with the East? And the dream also expressed one of our perennial Western anxieties. Does the East's focus on oneness represent some sort of wound to the head? Is it intellectually rigorous enough in its definition of individuality? How are we to safeguard our Western mind's attention to analysis and the distinction of the parts if we truly open to the oneness of the Mystery? And the dream, coming early on Easter morning with its three-times-repeated question, was calling me back to love, to love as the key to the way forward.

"Keep on reading 'Sleeping Beauty,'" said Bede. "Keep on reading 'Sleeping Beauty.'" The beauty of our oneness as a world can seem so distant that it is assumed dead, or so deeply forgotten that it is thought beyond recovery. How is the beauty of life's essential harmony to be reawakened? How is the curse of the spiteful divisions that have paralyzed us to be redeemed? In Grimm's fairy tale, the sleeping princess and her household are surrounded by age-old briars and thorns. Sleeping Beauty appears hopelessly beyond reach. The valiant princes who try to force their way through the hedge are consumed by the tangle of thorny briars. Only when the time is right does the hedge begin to open. And only with a kiss is Sleeping Beauty awakened.

We live in a moment of grace. Through the hedges of our divisions we are beginning to glimpse again the beauty of life's oneness. We are beginning to hear, in a way that humanity has never heard before, the essential harmony that lies at the heart of the universe. And we are beginning to understand, amidst the horror and the suffering of our divisions, that we will be well to the extent that we move back into relationship with one another, whether as individuals and families or as nations and species. The time is right. The time is desperately right. And it is only love that has the power to reawaken what has been paralyzed in our hearts. It is only the kiss of compassion that can re-member the beauty of our oneness. "Keep on reading 'Sleeping Beauty.' Keep on reading 'Sleeping Beauty.'"

PART TWO

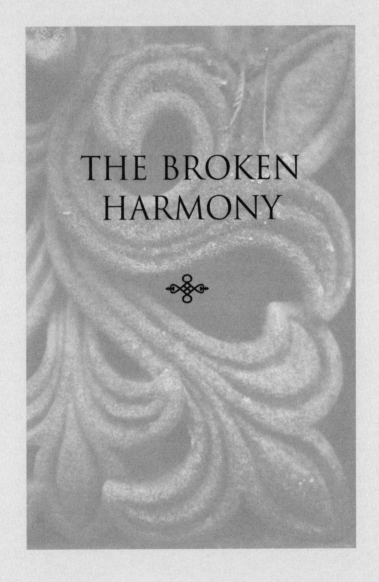

THE BROKEN HARMONY

CHAPTER 4

LOOKING SUFFERING STRAIGHT IN THE FACE

N oel O'Donoghue, the Carmelite mystic and philosopher from Ireland, used to say to us in our theology classes at the University of Edinburgh, "Life is a gift. But it is a gift shrouded in pain." There is an ancient harmony deep within the matter of the universe. All things carry within themselves the sound of the One. But the gift of life's essential harmony is broken. We hear only strains of it within us and between us as individuals and nations. The oneness of our relationship with the earth is broken by discord and suffering. The gift is shrouded in pain.

O'Donoghue also liked to tell the story of the renewal of baptismal vows in the south of Ireland where he grew up as a boy. When at the sacrament of baptism the priest would say to the people, "Do you renounce Satan and all his works?" the congregation would respond with heartfelt passion, "We do, the dirty bastard!" Not that this response ever made its way into written liturgical form!

But it is a response that speaks of passion in the face of wrong. Will there be change without it? The suffering that we witness in our families and children's lives. The divisions that we know between us as nations and religious traditions. The infections that are deep in the body of the earth and within us as creatures. Will any of this change if we avoid looking at it directly and compassionately—that is, with passion?

"I try to look things straight in the face."[1] These are the words of Etty Hillesum, a young Jewish woman who lived and died under the Nazi reign of terror in Holland during the Second World War. When the Netherlands capitulated to Germany in 1940, the Nazis began to isolate the Dutch Jews, throwing them out of their jobs, forbidding them from buying in stores frequented by non-Jews, requiring them to wear the yellow star to mark them as outcasts, and forcibly moving the Jewish population to designated ghettoes in Amsterdam so that the provinces could be declared judenrein (free of Jews). In May 1942, Etty wrote in her diary, "It is sometimes hard to take in and comprehend, oh God, what those created in Your likeness do to each other in these disjointed days. But I no longer shut myself away in my room. . . . I try to look things straight in the face, even the worst crimes."[2]

To look suffering in the face was part of Etty Hillesum's stature of soul. It allowed her to passionately name the falseness of what was happening all around her in Nazi-occupied Holland and, at the same time, to know that the battle was not simply an exterior one. It was being fought out also in the depths of her own soul. To look inhumanity in the face was to know that its madness could also take hold of her. She could capitulate to returning hatred for hatred and lose the struggle that each of us needs to be part of. "I feel like a small battlefield," she wrote, "in which the problems, or some of the problems, of our time are being fought out. All one can hope to do is to keep oneself humbly available, to allow oneself to be a battlefield."³ Life's essential harmony is within each of us. So also is life's brokenness. To be part of transformation is to look falseness in the face, to passionately name it and denounce it in our world, and at the same time to clearly identify its shadow within our own hearts and to do battle with it there.

I had a dream a few years ago, in which I tried to sneak into Carl Jung's tower house in Bollingen. In the dream, it had an exterior spiral staircase even though in reality the stairs are on the inside. In the dream, however, I was halfway up the tower heading for the top floor, which was Jung's place of solitude and study. It was a room into which very few people were invited. Thinking he was not in, I planned to creep into the room in his absence. So I was surprised when I heard his voice above me. "Come up," he said in his heavily accented English. I was embarrassed at being caught out, but delighted to be invited up.

The scene in the dream then changed. We were not in Jung's top-floor room but on the top of the tower itself, looking out in all directions. We had with us an ancient musical instrument, a precursor of the French horn, and we took it in turn to try to sound the lowest note possible. Finally, during one of Jung's attempts at the horn, I stood behind him and massaged his neck, thinking that if I could relax him, he would be able to produce the sound. Then it came, a full, clear vibrating of the lowest note. It resounded through us and all around us, traveling from the tower out into the surrounding woods.

Then, as if in response to the sound, there came people from the four directions. They were carrying what looked like ancient animal skins rolled up. They placed these at the foot of the tower—east, west, north, and south. Those who had carried the animal hides then unfurled them. Within each skin were human remains, thousands of years old. And it was clear that these human forbearers had died from violence, from ax wounds to the head or spear thrusts to the heart, from dismemberment and war.

The dream spoke to me of the depths of violence that we carry within us as a human species, as nations and religious traditions—layer upon layer of inherited violence. And it spoke of the capacity for violence in my own heart, in my thoughts and fears and struggles for survival. But the presence of Jung in the dream spoke also of healing, and especially of the relationship between consciousness and healing. He represented the desire to connect again with life's deepest note, the Sound that unites all things. And the dream spoke to me of the implicit relationship between knowing our true depths and knowing also the brokenness that is within us.

Knowing and naming brokenness is essential in the journey toward wholeness. We will not be well by denying the wrongs that we carry within us as nations and religions and communities. Nor will we be well by downplaying them or projecting them onto others. The path to wholeness will take us not around such awareness but through it, confronting the depths of our brokenness before being able to move forward toward healing. As Hildegard of Bingen says, we need two wings with which to fly. One is the "knowledge of good," and the other is the "knowledge of evil."[4] If we lack one or the other, we will be like an eagle with only one wing. We will fall to the ground instead of rising to the heights of unitary vision. We will live in half-consciousness instead of whole-consciousness.

The Lipchitz statue at the heart of the Roofless Church in New Harmony, *The Descent of the Spirit*, is a representation of the sacred womb from which life is born. It speaks of all things being conceived by the Spirit in the virgin womb of the universe. When Lipchitz first designed the piece, there was no lamb under the divine feminine form. It was only after a fire in his New York studio, which destroyed much of his work, that he decided to add the lamb. It is an image of innocence and of suffering. It is the lamb that will be slain. And in the Christian tradition it is the innocent one, the Christ-child, who will suffer.

So the Lipchitz statue grew. Its revised form spoke both of the sacredness of all matter, born from the *Mater*, as well as the pain and suffering of life. It is a statue that alludes to the continued slaughter of innocents in the world today. It invites us to remember the essential oneness and holiness of life and, at the same time, not to turn our faces away from the twenty thousand children who die every day from hunger-related disease. The presence of the lamb demands our attention. The innocent are vulnerable. The good suffer. The inclusion of the lamb does not allow us to turn from the truth of what we are doing or not doing to help the innocent ones of the world who suffer. It does not allow us to turn, for instance, from the fact that the $20 million we spend daily maintaining the U.S. nuclear arsenal, not to speak of the British and French and Israeli nuclear arsenals, could instead be used to provide $1,000 per day for every one of the twenty thousand children who die from hunger. Examples of such neglect are countless.

The Lipchitz statue speaks not just of the suffering of humanity but of the suffering of the creatures and the earth. The slaughter of innocents includes the extinction of three hundred species per week. We have viewed nonhuman life-forms as having no essential rights. Consequently our lifestyle is polluting the earth, and our greed is destroying the rain forests and the natural habitats that can no longer sustain the balance and integration of species that are necessary for our common well-being. We live in the midst of "an extinction spasm," as Thomas Berry calls it.[5] The nearly ten billion years that it took the universe to give birth to the earth, plus the four-and-a-half billion years of earth's unfolding diversity of life-forms, are being reversed in what is like the blink of an eye in earth's history. The last one hundred years have seen a massive degradation of the planet. The sacred gift of life is being slaughtered.

Julian of Norwich says there are three essential kinds of knowledge. The first is to know the One from whom all things have come. The second is to know ourselves and all life as made of the One. And the third is to know the true depths of our sinfulness or separateness from the One. Without the latter, our knowledge is not whole. Without a true awareness of the depths of brokenness, we will not find our way toward wholeness. "We do really need to see it," says Julian.[6] We do really need to look separateness and suffering straight in the face.

In one of her dreamlike awarenesses or visions of Jesus, Julian realizes that he is handsome. And the "handsome mixture" that she notes in him is "partly sorrow" and "partly joy."[7] His face speaks of a knowledge of life's delight and a knowledge of life's pain. It is not a face that is naive to the world's sufferings or to the personal experience of sorrow. Nor is it a face that is so overwhelmed by sorrow that it loses its openness and wonder. To be truly handsome, to be truly beautiful, is to reflect in one's countenance both life's glory and life's pain. It is not simply a sweet face, a pretty smile. It is a soul that has experienced the heights and the depths of human life.

One of my most handsome friends, in this sense of the word, is a former teacher of mine from the University of Edinburgh, Douglas Templeton. Always, even when I first knew him in my early student years, there was a beautiful combination in him of rugged good looks along with a countenance that was weather-beaten by life and with eyes that shone with sympathy. It was, I suppose, his sympathetic genius that freed him from having to tightly define belief. He was always able to see many sides to both belief and doubt. So much so that sometimes he was misunderstood as having no faith. The reality was that his belief in life was deep, but so deep that it was not easily expressed.

Douglas was known among his students at New College for sometimes not being able to find words for his complexity of thought. Sometimes halfway through a lecture he would pause, staring out the window, seeing some aspect of his subject matter that he had not seen before. And at such moments he would begin to say, "Yes. Yes. Yes. Yes." One class claimed to have counted over forty continuous yeses. I always found this to be part of his beauty. Life was not simply good. It was also wounded. The world was not simply a unity. It was also fragmented. Always there was more to be said about any perspective. And what cannot be said in life is always more important than what can be said.

On one occasion, Douglas and I were hiking in the Cairngorm Mountains along with an American student. We were making our way along the precipitous edge of Sgorn Dhu, one of the highest peaks in the Scottish Highlands. Its ridge falls suddenly into Glen Einich, a sheer drop of over one thousand feet. Douglas was in a state of awe at the grandeur of mountain expanse and the vastness of sky. For the last fifteen minutes of the walk he had been saying little more than "Yes." The American student and I were enjoying this mantra of praise when suddenly he shouted out "No!" Our friend thought Douglas was warning him about a rock slip, so he jumped like a kangaroo in the opposite direction. But Douglas was not warning him about a rock slip. He was saying no to something within himself, something that he was seeing that needed to be confronted. Within a few moments he was back to "Yes" again.

A deep "Yes" to life, to its wonder and sacred unity, is what we are all invited to utter in our hearts and lives. And an equally emphatic "No" is what we need to pronounce

and embody in our lives in the face of the world's deep
wrongs and sufferings. Over the last number of years,
Douglas has faced a place of suffering in his family's life
that is almost beyond imagining. It invites the strongest
"No" that any parent could utter. Three years ago his eldest
son, Alan, disappeared at the age of twenty-five. He has not
been seen since. There has not been a single trace. The
sorrow is unspeakable. And yet it is the sorrow of thousands
of families every year in our world, and it stands amidst a
plethora of sorrows in the human family and in the body
of the earth every day.

Douglas is truly handsome. Somehow, even though it is
difficult to fathom how, he holds joy in his face as well as
deep sorrow. To walk with him in the beautiful hills of the
Highlands or along the busy streets of a city is to experience
his "Yes" to life. He continues to gaze with wonder and
gratitude. And to share with him one's own struggles and
the pain of the world's journey is to know that he looks
deeply into the face of life. And thus he offers true strength
to the world and to others.

The same strength can be found in his wife, Elizabeth.
She also is a brilliant thinker and has played a creative role
in Scotland over the last thirty years as one of the nation's
first woman theologians. During a recent visit to their home
in the Highlands, Elizabeth, who has always been an appre-
ciator of my writings and of my focus on life's essential
sacredness, said to me, "I want you to write a book about
being battered by life."

I am not sure that I can do that. Partly it is because I
am not sure that I have the strength to focus on suffering

for so long. And partly it is because I believe that what we need is both the "Yes" and the "No" that Elizabeth and Douglas so beautifully embody in their journey. What we need is the "handsome mixture" of joy and sorrow that Julian saw in the face of Jesus. What we need are the two wings, the awareness of good and the awareness of evil, that Hildegard saw was necessary if we are to rise to a redemptive way of seeing. This will take us not around our sorrow but through it. This combination will look life's brokenness straight in the face in order that we may see the way forward.

I never knew my grandfather on my father's side of the family. James Newell died before I was born. I grew up not knowing much about him. And I have come to realize that there is much about my grandfather that even my father never knew. James Newell left Belfast when my father was just an infant. He sailed to Canada to make his way in the New World, leaving behind my grandmother with three children—a son and two daughters. My father, William James, was not to meet his father again until he was eight years old.

When the family reunited in Canada, it seems that there were aspects of the family that would never truly unite. My grandmother was a devout Plymouth Brethren, and my grandfather an atheistic socialist. And during his long spell alone in Canada, he had entered an illicit relationship, fathering children with another woman. Although this was not known to my father at the time, he grew up under the shadow of an unhappy marriage. The early 1930s was a time

of economic hardship for the family, my father as a boy
having to walk the railway lines to find pieces of discarded
coal from passing freight trains in order to heat the family
home for his mother and sisters over the long Canadian
winters. And Sundays were a day of great tension. His
mother wanted to take him to church, and the father whom
he hardly knew wanted to treat him to the cinema.

I grew up knowing next to nothing about my Grandfather
Newell. He was hidden in a shroud of secrecy. My father as
a boy chose at some level to side with his mother, under-
standably. What I was able to glimpse of James Newell in
family lore was of a largely undefined character. My father
was too loyal to say much about him, and perhaps too
ashamed. So I knew very little. Until, that is, I got involved
in Canadian politics in the summer of 1984. Ali and I
were living in Hamilton at the time, close to where my
father had emigrated in 1930. And I was persuaded to run
for office as a member of Parliament in the Canadian federal
election.

My grandfather too had been involved in Canadian
politics. He was a founding member of the Canadian Cooper-
ative Federation. He too had run for office in Hamilton
and had been elected as a local councillor at the municipal
level. I knew the bare outlines of his political career,
but nothing much more than that. Yet as I knocked on
doors in the constituency of Hamilton West in the hot
summer of 1984, I began to meet old men who would
look me in the face and then look at my nametag and say,
"Philip Newell. You're not related to James Newell, are you?"
And within no time at all I had more stories about my

grandfather than I had ever had in my life. They were stories
of color and passion, of him getting involved in fistfights at
street corners over political debate, of him arguing for just
political reform in the debates of City Hall, of him gener-
ously lending money to other families in need. And I began
to see that he was more than just a scallywag. He was a man
of passionate vision. That summer I claimed something of
my grandfather deep in my heart. Amid the veiled, and later
explicit, references to his faithlessness and his irreligion, I
was able to see the goodness of the man.

Many years later, I was leading a pilgrimage on Iona. I
had been struggling for some time with a sore shoulder that
was referring pain up into my neck and lower head. Nothing,
in terms of therapy, was touching it. I could find no sustained relief from the discomfort. I mentioned this to one
of the participants on the retreat. She was a Reike therapist
and offered to try to help. During our first session, she
explained that we could begin the therapy by invoking the
love of those who had gone before me in my life. She asked
if I was thinking about anyone in particular. The name that
immediately came to mind was James Newell, my grandfather. The therapist did not ask for any details about him
but simply explained that we carry within us the life of
those who have gone before and that part of what we carry
within us is their brokenness. But as well as their brokenness, she said, we carry their love and their desire for our
wholeness.

Her words further opened up for me the awareness that
some of the pain that we carry, whether in our bodies or
in our psyches, is not simply ours. Some of it comes from

those who have gone before us, just as some of it comes also from other human beings and other creatures and elements of creation with whom we are in relationship. Some of what I carried within me was from my grandfather. The Reike therapist encouraged me to be conscious of this and to know that part of my pain was his pain. She encouraged me also to be aware that my grandfather desired my well-being. And at the end of our time together on Iona, she suggested a discipline that I had never heard of nor ever contemplated practicing. She suggested that for the next two weeks I set aside a time every evening to light a candle in my room at home in order to have a prayerful imaginary conversation with my grandfather.

And that is what I did. Every evening, I would sit and prayerfully imagine my grandfather for about twenty minutes. In my imagination, I would ask him about his life, about his strengths and confusions, about his delight in life and his sorrow. And in silence I would listen. I did not of course receive more information about James Newell during those times of silence. There is so much that we still do not know about him and maybe will never know. We do not even know his place of birth or his father's name. He was born out of wedlock and probably never knew his own father. That is part of the pain that he carried. And that is part of the pain that my father has carried, and that I carry, and that my sons will carry.

I did not receive more historical detail about my grandfather during those evenings of prayerful imagination. I did, however, come to know him in a new way. And I came to know myself in a new way. I was looking things more directly in the face. I was looking at the brokenness of his life, and it drew me into deeper relationship with him. No longer was I primarily judging him or perplexed by him. I felt compassion, a passion for him and a passion with him. I was looking at his brokenness and my brokenness, at our brokenness.

My shoulder pain did not suddenly disappear. But this time was an important stage of healing for me. I now realized, especially when I lay in bed after my prayerful evenings with my grandfather, that I felt a type of kindness toward the pain in my shoulder instead of only annoyance or impatience at the discomfort. It was in part my grandfather's pain, not just my pain. The way forward was different because I was seeing with different eyes. And something in me knew that my grandfather desired my well-being just as I desire my sons' well-being. I was looking at our shared brokenness more directly. And to know something of its source and its origin was strengthening for me.

Jung says that "history is not contained in thick books but lives in our very blood."[8] If we wish to know the source of brokenness in our world, whether as individuals or nations, we need to look at what we carry within us. And some of what is within us was already deeply present in the lives of our ancestors. The less we understand our fathers and our mothers, the less we will understand ourselves. The essential interwovenness of life means that to look suffering in the face is to look deeply into our own face and in our own face to see the faces of those who have gone before us. Edwin Muir, the Scottish poet, calls it "the face once broken in Eden."[9] It is the face deep within every human being.

⋅⊰⧈⊱⋅

In July 1942, the same month that the Nazis began their first big street roundups of Jews in Amsterdam, Etty Hillesum wrote in her diary, "I am with the hungry, with the ill-treated and the dying, every day, but I am also with the jasmine and with the piece of sky beyond my window. . . . It is a question of living life from minute to minute and taking suffering into the bargain. And it is certainly no small bargain these days."[10] Etty was looking at suffering straight in the face. Her friends, her family, and she herself were under the sentence of extermination. It was now beginning to be carried out. And yet Etty held within herself the "handsome mixture" of pain at the plight of her people, and of what one people can do to another people, along with a continued delight in the gift of life and its ineffable wonder. "I have looked our destruction, our miserable end, which has already begun in so many small ways in our daily life, straight in the eye," she writes, "and my love of life has not been diminished."[11] To look life straight in the eye, to see its pain and to see its beauty—this is an essential part of glimpsing the way forward.

CHAPTER 5

DIGGING GOD OUT

I n July 1942, the Nazis set in motion their first big street roundup of Jews in Amsterdam. The plan was to concentrate the Jewish population in Westerbork, a transit camp in the east of the Netherlands, not far from the German border. Though not itself an extermination camp, Westerbork would be the last stop before Auschwitz for more than one hundred thousand Dutch Jews over the next three years. The twenty-eight-year-old Etty Hillesum was temporarily immune from arrest because she worked for the Cultural Affairs Department of the Jewish Council. Nevertheless, in a desire to be with her persecuted brother and sister Jews, she volunteered to work in the camp at Westerbork.

"I love people so terribly," she wrote in her diary in the form of a prayer, "because in every human I love something of You [O God]. And I seek You everywhere in them and often do find something of You."[1] Westerbork had originally been built by the Dutch government to house fifteen hundred German Jews who had fled to the Netherlands before the war. But when Etty arrived at Westerbork in

the summer of 1942, the Nazis had turned it into a
transit camp in which they were holding over thirty thousand Jews en route to extermination in the gas chambers of
Poland. It was a crowded community of men, women, and
children living in fear, degradation, and the dread of what
lay ahead.

Every Tuesday a train would leave the camp for
Auschwitz. The long line of freight cars was packed with
over a thousand people each time. Amidst the horror of
what was happening, Etty was aware of what she called
a "repose" in the deepest part of her being.[2] And she
looked for that place of strength in the deepest part of
those around her. "The most essential and the deepest in
me," she wrote, "hearkening unto the most essential and
deepest in the other. God to God."[3] Even before arriving at
the camp, she had spoken of a well deep inside every human
being in which God dwells. But so often the inner well is
blocked with stones and grit, she said, and God is buried.
"He must be dug out again."[4] How do we dig God out?
How in our lives individually and in the midst of the
unspeakable wrongs that our nations are part of, how do
we release that deepest part of our being, that part which
Etty calls "God"?

New Harmony, Indiana, became again a place of vision
after the Second World War. The rebirth of vision was associated with the teachings of Paul Tillich, who as a young
German theologian fled Nazi Europe to find sanctuary in
the United States. Tillich is perhaps best known for his vision
of God as "ground of being."[5] It is a term that prophetically
anticipated the earth awareness that we are in the midst of

today. It is a way of seeing that brought balance to the notion of transcendence that had dominated much of our Western Christian inheritance. For Tillich, the Transcendent One is the Immanent One. We will find the heights of the Mystery by delving into the depths of the universe and the human soul. We will seek the holy not by looking away from life but by penetrating the very heart of life. The invitation is to dig into the Ground of our being. The challenge is to open up again the well that lies hidden within everything that has being.

Jane Owen of New Harmony found in Tillich the articulation of what she was already intuiting through her artistic sensibilities—that the sacred is to be found within the human form and within the body of the earth. Tillich provided words for where the Spirit was already leading her. The decision to build the Roofless Church, opening onto the vastness of creation, was part of opening again to the holy well within all things. The commissioning of the Lipchitz statue, *The Descent of the Spirit*, was part of declaring again that everything in the universe is begotten of God.

At the opposite end of the Roofless Church from *The Descent of the Spirit* is another sculpture, *The Pieta*, by Stephen de Staebler. It is the primitive form of a woman standing naked. Her breast is split open. And from within her breast appears the head of her crucified son. In the palms of her hands, and in her feet and sides, are the nail-marks of crucifixion. She is Mary the Mother. She is every mother who has lost her child. She is the mother parted from her son in the transit camp of Westerbork. She is the mother of the disappeared in El Salvador. She is the mother of starving children in the Sudan. And the pain that she knows in her brokenness is not an exterior pain. It does not come primarily from without. It issues up from the very heart of her being.

Part of digging God out is releasing the woundedness of God. Part of believing in the Ground of being is to name the sorrow that issues up from the deepest part of our being when our child suffers, when earth's species are crucified, when the people and the nations we love are wronged. And for Jane Owen this was not a theoretical insight. She had tragically lost one of her own daughters to death. Rarely did she speak about it. Her intention in commissioning The Pieta was not to draw attention to her own pain. It was to release the sound of God's woundedness in our pain. It was, as Etty Hillesum said, to "hearken" to the depths of the other. It was to believe that we will find the way forward in our lives and world not by ignoring or playing down the agony of earth's journey or the pain of our particular paths but by hearing the sacredness of the cry.

There is another sculpture at the east end of the Roofless Church. It sits in relationship to The Pieta and is called The Polish Memorial, by Eva Sygulka. It remembers the pain of a whole nation—Poland under Nazi occupation. The sculpture is of God as Father. He is behind the crucified one, supporting with his own arms the outstretched arms of his son on the cross. The Father is the deep strength of the son. It was typical of Jane Owen to balance the feminine sculpture, The Pieta, with a representation of the masculine, The Polish Memorial. She was forever seeking to hold in relationship what has been torn apart. She was forever insisting, like Jung, that the way to wholeness is to be found by conjoining what has been considered opposite—the masculine and the feminine, the life of one people and the life of another, the night and the day, the conscious and the unconscious.

Jane Owen knew that if we are to be healed, we must release the sacred sound of our pain—the cry of the mother in us at the agony of life's brokenness. She also believed that if we are to be strong in our brokenness, we must know that we are supported. Often she would walk in the Roofless Church in the mornings and evenings and "happen" to meet parents who had lost their child or individuals in the midst of grief and struggle. She was discreet about her own pain and would never pry into the lives of those she met praying in the Roofless Church. But when she did learn their stories, she was deeply present to them, often holding their hands, allowing the cry of their journey to be heard. And, like Etty Hillesum, she would offer strength to them by bringing the most essential and deepest part of herself to the most essential and deepest part of the other, "God to God."

This is what Jane Owen did for me the first time we met. She had read my book Listening for the Heartbeat of God, in which there is a chapter devoted to George MacLeod, whom she loved as a friend and teacher. She sensed in my writings a continuity with his vision, so she invited me to teach in New Harmony. On that first occasion, I was seated in the Red Geranium restaurant finishing an evening meal with others when Jane Owen, by that stage in her mideighties, entered. She was a beautiful woman, bearing in her countenance the combination of which Julian of Norwich speaks, a countenance partly of joy and partly of sorrow. When I stood to greet her, she took my hands in hers and closed her eyes, that posture she would adopt when listening deeply. Among her first questions to me was, "How is your family?" She did not yet know that my Brendan had become unwell in a tortuous struggle with mental illness, an illness that affects so many of our families today, an illness that is symptomatic of our world's brokenness. When Jane Owen learned of my Brendan's pain, her eyes moistened with compassion.

I knew that my pain as a father had been heard by her. And I knew that it was not just my pain. It was Jane Owen's pain. It was the pain of countless families. It was the pain of the world. Naming it, expressing it, allowing it to be heard is essential on the pathway toward healing. This is why the Roofless Church's Pieta is so powerful. But what I did not yet perceive, and only came to fully comprehend years later during my sabbatical stay in New Harmony, was that The Pieta and The Polish Memorial belong inseparably together. Yes, it is essential that the sacred cry of brokenness be heard, and to know that that cry comes from the divine depths of the Ground of being within us. But equally essential is to know the strength of God in the depths of our being. As the Scriptures say, "Underneath are the everlasting arms" (Deuteronomy 33:27).

In the spring of 2010, I preached at the fiftieth anniversary of the Roofless Church. It was a great moment for celebrating anew the vision of God's vast and untamable presence, and the wild geese flying past us during the service honked their approval. In my homily, however, I made reference to *The Pieta*. I spoke of our need to fully face the brokenness of our lives and world. But I failed to mention *The Polish Memorial*. And in that sense I failed to address the question that most haunts us in much of our brokenness: Where is our strength to be found?

Jane Owen was still with us for the fiftieth anniversary celebrations. She died the following month. But at the age of ninety-five she was gloriously alive that day. As we processed into the Roofless Church together, I was preoccupied with my coming homily, focusing straight ahead. She, in contrast, was smiling at people from side to side as we walked down the central aisle. Her version of it later on, however, was that she was counting the numbers! Jane Owen appreciated my sermon, but the next day she found a way of letting me know what I had missed. In commenting on *The Polish Memorial*, she said, "But we are supported in our suffering."

We are supported, even in what can seem like the hopelessness of our pain. In *The Polish Memorial*, the Father is the strength that holds up the outstretched arms of the son. In the agony of a whole nation, in the individual agonies of our lives, in the agony of the earth's suffering, there is strength to be found. It is what Etty Hillesum calls the place of "repose." It is the place deep within where we may reposition ourselves, where we may find our true balance, our ultimate stability. What is the suffering in our lives today? Do we know that there is a well of strength for us? What is the suffering in those around us and in our world? Do we know that there is sacred strength in us for them? And do

we know that we can dig deep within ourselves and one
another to find the Strength that is deeper than us all?
"Underneath are the everlasting arms."

What is it that happened in the life of the Polish nation
during the Second World War? The German nation, under
Nazi leadership, had raised itself up over another people.
And not only did the Nazis deeply wrong the Polish people,
but they used the sovereign land of Poland to perpetrate on
European Jewry some of the deepest wrongs that humanity
has known. The German nation was not alone in this. Some
of our worst inhumanities as nations, including Britain and
America, have been perpetrated on foreign soil and kept at
a distance, as if to hide from our own soul the sacrilege of
what we are doing. When we lift ourselves up over the holy
sovereignty of another nation, something in us has known
that the violence we inflict on another people would never
be tolerated by the conscience of our own people if it were
done nearer home. And something in our collective psyche
has pretended that the families of another land are not as
sacred as the sons and daughters of our own.

The Quran includes a powerful account of the creation
of humanity. When God brings forth humanity from the
fecundity of the earth, the divine command to the holy
angels is to bow down and honor what has been made in
the holy image. The angels prostrate themselves before
Adam and Eve, with one exception. The greatest angel,
the angel of light, refuses to bow. He says he will not
bow to what comes out of the earth, out of "the black
moulded loam" of earth's soil (Al-Hijr 15:28). And thus
begins the falseness of Satan. He chooses the path of hubris,

of lifting himself up over the earth, of positioning himself above the other.

Think of the hubris of our lives. Think of our individual arrogance, the way we pursue our own well-being at the neglect and even expense of other individuals and other families. Think of the hubris of our nationhood, pretending that we could look after the safety of our homeland by ignoring and even violating the sovereignty of other lands. Think of the hubris of our religion, raising ourselves up over other wisdom traditions and even trying to force our ways on them. Think of the hubris of the human species, pretending that we could look after our own health while exploiting and endangering the life of other species.

The way of hubris, of arrogantly lifting ourselves up over the other, is opposite to the way of Jesus, who taught the strength of humility, of being close to the humus, close to the Ground from which we and all things come. The humblest, says Jesus, are "the greatest" (Matthew 18:4). Not that following Jesus' path of humility is straightforward. Constantly there is tension—the tension of discerning how to love our neighbor as we love ourselves, how to honor the heart of another nation as we honor our own homeland, how to revere the truths of another wisdom tradition as we cherish our own inheritance, how to protect the life of other species as we guard the sanctity of our own life-form. Jesus knew such tension. He was tempted to use his wisdom and his power of presence to serve himself, to lift himself up over others. But to the tempter, he says, "Away with you, Satan!" (Matthew 4:10). Away with the falseness of believing that I can love myself and demean others.

The twelfth-century teacher Hildegard of Bingen says, "Arrogance is always evil because it oppresses everything, disperses everything, and deprives everything."[6] The way of hubris pretends that we can be well by oppressing, by exploiting another people in order to serve our own people. It pretends that we can be well by dispersing, by breaking down life's oneness into entirely unrelated compartments. And it pretends that we can be well by depriving, by denying to others and to other species what we ourselves most cherish. "By way of contrast," says Hildegard, "humility does not rob people or take anything from them. Rather, it holds together everything in love."[7] The way of humility, of reconnecting to the humus, remembers the sacred Ground of being within us all. And it knows that we will be truly well to the extent that we love one another.

In the Quran, Satan refuses to bow to what comes out of the earth. This seventh-century story points to the heart of much of our brokenness today. We have refused to honor what comes out of the earth—our bodies, the life of every nation, the origin of every species, the sacredness of our natural resources, the oneness from which life comes. Eriugena in the ninth century says that falseness is "that which seeks to be what it is not."[8] We have forgotten who we are, born of the earth. We have lived the delusion of thinking that we could pollute the earth and not pollute our souls. We have believed the lie that we could be happy and ignore the hunger of others. We have followed the falseness of seeking to be something other than what we truly are—one with the earth, part of every life-form.

The word sin comes from the Old High German *sunda*, which means "to sunder" or "to tear apart." Think of the sunderings we have been part of as nations, as individuals, as a species. Jung says that the devil's nature is "binary."[9] It seeks to divide unity into duality. It attempts to tear apart what belongs together. From one it is always trying to make two—heaven and earth, spirit and matter, the feminine and the masculine, the night and the day, the conscious and the unconscious, the heart and the head, spirituality and sexuality, the East and the West, the one and the many, the life of humanity and the life of the whole of creation.

Teilhard de Chardin, the twentieth-century scientist and priest, describes sin as slowing down or dividing the essential unity of the universe. In cosmic terms, he says, it is "counter-evolution."[10] Rather than seeing reality as a web of interrelated influences, in which the essential unity of life is forever expressing itself in greater and greater diversity, we participate in sin or sundering when we forget the organic unity of the whole and treat the distinct parts as disparate. In evolutionary terms, if humanity forgets its essential interdependence with the earth, it will lead not to the further flowering of humanity but to the depletion of humanity. If we sunder what belongs together—the life of humanity and the life of earth's other species, the well-being of one people and the well-being of every people, the wisdom of one tradition and the teachings of other great traditions—we will experience the judgment of sin, or what we might prefer to call the consequences of sundering. We are already in the midst of judgment for what we are doing to the earth. We are already experiencing the consequences of our divisions as nations and religions. The cost of sundering is self-destruction. Or, as the Scriptures say, "the wages of sin is death" (Romans 6:23). It is the same reality whichever way we put it. But this is not a judgment imposed on us from without. This is a consequence being experienced by us from within. The law of the universe is love. To the extent that we disregard it, we imperil our very existence.

The fourteenth-century mystic Meister Eckhart taught that to not love another is to not love oneself. "As long as you love one single person less than yourself," he said, "you have never really loved yourself."[11] So much are we one that what we do to another is what we do to ourselves. So much are we one, said Eckhart, that "all division is division from the one."[12] The way of sin or sundering, he said, is about "non-being."[13] It is about moving toward nonexistence. To separate myself from another through hatred is to murder something within myself. To sunder the life of our nation from the life of another nation is to deplete the very life source of our own nation. To isolate the wisdom of our religious inheritance from the spirituality of other peoples is to malnourish our own children's souls. To detach the well-being of our species from the well-being of all earth's species is to threaten the very future of our species. "As long as you love one single person less than yourself, you have never really loved yourself."

The more we sin or sunder, the more we assume that the parts are unrelated to the whole and that we can be well while ignoring the well-being of others. The more we sin or sunder, the more addicted we become to the convenience of a fragmented universe in which all we need to do is look after our own patch. It is like a drunken state in which we more and more fall out of touch with reality. And the less we are in touch with reality, the more we want to drink, the more we want to escape the deepest realities of life as interwoven.

I have known alcoholism in members of my own family. I have seen drunkenness eat away at the true core of another's beauty, at the true core of another's ability to discern, at the true core of another's desire for relationship. I have seen it sunder family members from one another. And the disease that may have been caused by inherited family sunderings or social deprivations ends up multiplying the brokenness over and over again. I witnessed my aunt physically shrivel up through alcohol abuse. And nearly everything about her shriveled—her network of friends, her family support, her outlook on life, her capacity to be truthful, and finally her will to live. I watched my father's agony as he lost his sister over many years. There was nothing he could do. She was never willing to name her brokenness. And she never believed that there was a deeper Strength, although sometimes in her drunken state it seemed she was calling out for that Strength.

How do we pull out of our drunkenness? How do we reverse the spirals of delusion within us, whether as individuals or as nations, in which we have come to believe that we are essentially separate from one another? How do we stop the cycle of addiction and our attempts to escape reality? And what is it that will enable us to fully name the extent of our brokenness and open to the place of "repose," as Etty Hillesum puts it, that place deep within the Ground of our being in which we can radically reposition ourselves, that place from which to dig out again our strength to love so that we can move back into relationship with one another and with all things?

During our student years, Ali and I lived in community in an Edinburgh slum. The beautiful capital of Scotland has tucked its poverty away into corners of the city where visitors, and even other Edinburgh residents, need never pass. The worst of the city's social brokenness is hidden. We were young students at the time and, with ten others, rented six apartments on a common stair at the heart of Pilton, in those years one of Edinburgh's worst pockets of social and economic deprivation. The idea was simply to be in a part of the city that had been forgotten and neglected. Most of us worked or studied elsewhere in Edinburgh, but Pilton was home. Our commitment was to live there and to engage in the neighborhood. Our only simple rule of community life was to meditate and pray together every evening and to share a common meal on Sundays.

These were happy and challenging years. Many of us on the stair were young couples, and it was here that we began our families. We in fact produced so many babies in the first couple of years that word got round in Pilton that we were a fertility cult! There was Killer the dog who lived a few doors along. As his name would suggest, he had not been trained with friendly intent. Killer particularly liked passing cyclists and would attack us from the most unexpected hiding places each day as we cycled past. And there was

Jimmy our neighbor, a rotund little man who was rumored to have fathered over twenty children in the area. Every few days a cartload of lemonade bottles would arrive at his door. A few hours later Jimmy would emerge with two cartloads of lemonade bottles for resale. In the meantime he had watered down the original supply.

But amidst the comedy of life in Pilton there was deep tragedy. One of our neighbors was alcoholic. He was a quiet man who would faithfully go off to work every weekday morning and come back in time for his evening meal. But on Fridays he would not return until the middle of the night—drunk and violent. Through the walls we would hear his wife screaming and the sound of furniture being smashed. On Saturdays we would hear nothing. Then on Sundays only the sound of his hammer repairing the broken furniture. Cycles of drunkenness. Spirals of sundering. How are we to reverse them?

"The most essential and the deepest in me," wrote Etty Hillesum, "hearkening unto the most essential and deepest in the other. God to God." Although we did not have the beauty and depth of Etty's language to speak in these terms, this is what we were searching for in our Pilton years. We had a sense of wanting to be in relationship with Pilton's brokenness, sharing its life, choosing not to separate ourselves from its journey, although of course part of us was always separate anyway. We knew we could move on at any time. And this was not the reality for most of Pilton's residents. But something in us wanted to open to them. And we knew there was something in us to offer. The real surprise for us was how much we received.

It was initially the children of the neighborhood who got to know us. Others were cautiously perplexed as to why we would choose to live in Pilton. But the children were immediately interested and simply enjoyed our presence. They would knock on our doors after school. Sometimes it was just to have a word—someone to speak to, someone to listen to them. Other times it was to come in for a snack—a quiet place, a type of sanctuary in their often chaotic lives. But the problem was that we had other things to do as well. I was trying to write my PhD thesis. Others were hoping that their baby's afternoon nap would not every day be cut short by children knocking at the door. So we had a bright idea. Each day we would place a star on a different door in the stair. And the children on our street were told that they could knock on the door with the star but not on the other doors. It was a brilliant idea. By the third day of the experiment, however, word had got round at the local school with its hundreds of children that we were running an after-school club. Go to the apartment with the star! Hordes of children came.

We had to downscale our operation, but over the years there were numbers of children who became close to us. Some of them would even join us for evening prayer. Who knows what they received from it, but there must have been an attractive combination in the stillness and welcome and the cup of sweet tea at the end. Our most regular visitor for evening prayer was James. He was an unusual-looking boy. His eyes were crossed, which always made it difficult to know where he was looking. His hands and face were unwashed, and the pungent smell of his clothes from a household full of cats and dogs that were rarely let out made it difficult to be in close proximity to him.

One evening, James arrived late for community prayer. Ali and I had placed a copy of Rublev's icon of Mother and Child on the mantelpiece above the hearth. The community was seated in a semicircle, prayerfully meditating in silence on the icon. The only remaining seat for James was a little stool in front of the fireplace. But when he sat down, he did not face the icon with the rest of us. Instead, he faced us. Perhaps he did not know what we were doing. And maybe his eyesight was not good enough to see what our focus was. But he began to smile at us. And the more he smiled at us, the more our focus shifted from the icon to James, until eventually his countenance became the icon. It was a window into the face of God. The most essential and the deepest in us gazing into the most essential and the deepest in James. We were digging God out in one another.

During the time that Etty Hillesum was still permitted to travel in and out of the transit camp at Westerbork, she spurned all attempts by her Amsterdam friends to hide her in a safe house in the city. And later, when she was no longer allowed to leave the camp, she rejected all offers of help to escape. She was determined to be with her people in the midst of their agony. "I shall try to help You, God," she wrote in her diary.[14] Increasingly she knew that what really mattered was to safeguard what she called that "little piece" of God in herself and in those around her.[15] "Alas, there doesn't seem to be much You Yourself can do about our circumstances," she prayed, "but we must help You and defend Your dwelling place inside us to the last."[16] This she realized is the only way of really helping, by digging deep within ourselves and within one another to release God from the hidden depths of our soul.

CHAPTER 6

A BALM FOR
ALL WOUNDS

No one in the Westerbork transit camp had heard about the gas chambers of Auschwitz, but Etty Hillesum and others knew in their hearts that there would be no return from the train journey to Poland. "When the first transport passed through our hands," wrote Etty after the departure of the earliest consignment of Jews from Westerbork to Auschwitz, "there was a moment when I thought I would never again laugh. . . . But on walking through the crowded camp, I realized again that where there are people, there is life."[1]

In the camp hospital where she cared for the sick, many of whom would soon find their names on the transportation list, and in her barracks at night where she would hear the sobbing of women in the dark and the tormented cries of others in their sleep, Etty looked into the agony of soul that she was in the midst of. She knew fear in her own heart and witnessed it taking hold of others and driving them to hatred. "I know that those who hate have good reason to do so," she wrote. "But why should we always have to choose the cheapest and easiest way?"[2]

This is not to say that wrestling with revulsion at her captors was foreign to Etty. She describes looking at the faces of the armed guards who were loading her fellow Jews onto the next train for Auschwitz. "I looked at them, each in turn, from behind the safety of a window, and I have never been so frightened of anything in my life. I sank to my knees with the words that preside over human life: 'And God made man after His likeness.' That passage spent a difficult morning with me."[3]

Etty believed that each of us needs to destroy within ourselves all that we think we ought to destroy in others. First and foremost is the conflict with hatred in our own hearts. We need "to reclaim large areas of peace in ourselves," she wrote. "And the more peace there is in us, the more peace there will also be in our troubled world."[4] In the autumn of 1942, having witnessed thousands upon thousands being herded into the weekly freight cars bound for Poland, and having endured months of the degradation imposed on her people, she wrote, "We should be willing to act as a balm for all wounds."[5] This is what she was doing physically in her work in the camp hospital. It was also at the heart of her relationship with those around her in Westerbork and in her continued correspondence with friends in Amsterdam, who felt powerless to arrest the nightmare of their nation. "We should be willing to act as a balm for all wounds."

Carl Jung says that "the whole world is God's suffering."[6] The woundedness is everywhere. We know it both individually and collectively. It is in the cells of our souls and the atoms of the universe. It is in our genetic code and

the inherited memory of our families. It is deep in the life
of the earth and the history of every nation. It is a woundedness that is both intensely personal and unlimitedly vast.
The one does not occur without the other. They are inseparably related. And their healing also is indissolubly one.

Jung noticed in his psychoanalytical work with patients,
and observed also in the journey of his own soul, that a
collective human problem will often manifest itself powerfully as a personal problem. He concluded that our focus
must be twofold: to compassionately treat the individuality
of our wounds and at the same time tend the collective
brokenness of our world. In the midst of treating the fears
that haunt our minds individually, and the mental illness
and collapse of relationship that characterize our family
lives, we are to passionately address the brokenness of
our nations and the woundedness of the earth. Our personal
problems will not be sorted by neglecting our collective problems. And the reverse also is true. We will not
heal the earth's brokenness by ignoring our individual
brokenness.

In 1913 Jung noted a growing darkness and depression
in his own psyche. By October of that year, he even saw
within himself images of a terrible flood. It was like an
ominous catastrophe waiting to happen. In his psyche he
saw "the floating rubble of civilization," "drowned bodies,"
and a "whole sea turned to blood."[7] A number of months
later, the First World War broke out. Jung now understood
what his life task was to be. "I had to try to understand . . .
to what extent my own experience coincided with that of
mankind in general."[8] He felt compelled to know the rela-

tionship between the one and the many, the personal and the collective, the depths of what we experience individually and the river that runs deep in the human soul.

When I stand in Carol's Garden in New Harmony, dedicated to the memory of Jane Owen's daughter Carol, I think of the wound of Jane Owen's sorrow as a mother. I also think of my own family's wounds and the sorrow of families throughout the world today. I think of the brokenness of whole nations and species. Thomas Berry calls it "the deep pathos of the Earth situation," the pain that is not limited to one person or one nation or one species.[9] Carol's Garden, which is circular, has at its heart a font of perpetual light and an unending flow of water. The Bradford pears that have been planted in concentric circles all lean toward the center of the garden. They have been trained with taut wires to incline inward toward the font.

Jung, quoting from an ancient hermetic source, says, "God is a circle whose center is everywhere and the circumference is nowhere."[10] Wherever we look, into whoever's eyes we gaze, into whichever life-form we peer, into whatever family or nation we move, there is the heart of God. And there also is the suffering of God. Our traditions have often tried to place fixed-circumference walls around the sacred—whether that be the sacredness of our religion, the sacredness of our nation, or the sacredness of our species. But the sacredness is everywhere. As is the woundedness of God. New science has given us the ability to conceive that we live in an omnicentric universe. There is no such thing as one central point to the cosmos. Every point is the center, for the universe expands infinitely in all directions. When I stand in Carol's Garden, I am aware of the font at the heart of life. It is at the heart of every moment and every place. And I am aware also of the wound that is everywhere to be found. How are we to seek wholeness?

A few summers ago at our little retreat center in New Mexico, we were exploring themes of wholeness. We were asking how the broken harmony of our lives and world can be transformed. What does the transformation from wound-edness to wholeness look like, whether individually or among us as nations and species? Among the participants at our retreat was a couple from Colorado, Larry and Diane. A number of months earlier, they had lost their son, Zach, in an airplane crash. They opened their hearts to us as a group and allowed us to share in their grieving. When it came time in our reflections to ask what it means to seek transforma-tion, and how we are to move from brokenness toward wholeness, Larry said simply and unforgettably, "If by wholeness you mean some sort of smoothing over of the gaping wound that will always be in me because of my son's death, I don't want that sort of wholeness."

Larry was not meaning that he wanted forever to be paralyzed by his son's death. He was not meaning that he did not wish to move toward transformation. He was meaning, however, that he wished never to forget the pre-ciousness of his son's life and his agony as a father in losing Zach. And he was meaning that any true journey of trans-formation would not skirt around that wound but would incorporate it deeply into whatever the new beginning was to be. When he finished speaking, he reminded us of the resurrection story in St. John's Gospel. The risen Jesus, he said, shows the disciples the marks of crucifixion in his hands and side. The resurrection story is not about the wounds being undone. It is not about the suffering being smoothed over. The wounds are deeply visible. They are part of the new beginning. They are an inseparable part of the new beginning.

Jung says that wholeness is about "integration . . . but not perfection."[11] It is about bringing into relationship again the many parts of our lives, including our brokenness, in order to experience transformation. It is not about forgetting the wound or pretending that it did not happen. It is about seeking a new beginning that grows inseparably out of the suffering. It is not about returning to Eden, an unblemished state of innocence within us or between us. It is about bringing our origin in Eden, the root that connects us still to the sacredness of our beginnings, into the depths of our exile from Eden, including all of the woundedness that false decisions and wrong turns have created within us and between us in our lives.

As the Scottish poet Kenneth White writes, this is not "any kind of easy harmonization."[12] It is not about returning to a simple unspoiled melody. It is about seeking a new harmony that fully recognizes the experience and the depth of our brokenness. Or as Edwin Muir, another Scottish poet, put it in his poem "One Foot in Eden," it is about seeking a blossom that was "never known" in Eden.[13] "What," he asks, "had Eden ever to say of hope and faith and pity and love?" These, he says, are "strange blessings" to Eden. They come not simply out of the garden of our beginnings. They are born out of the "grief" and "darkened fields" of our lives.[14]

What is the "grief" in our lives today? And what are the "darkened fields" of our world in which it appears that no good can come? The fourteenth-century mystic Julian of Norwich in her *Revelations of Divine Love* hears the assurance that "all shall be well, and all shall be well, and all manner of things shall be well."[15] This is not naive optimism in Julian. Her revelations, or "perceptions" as she also calls them, are full of the awareness of suffering.[16] She herself lies ill during her revelations, appearing to those around her to be on her deathbed. She sees so much blood in her dreamlike awarenesses of Christ that at one point she says that if it had been real blood, her bed would have been flowing like a stream.

"All shall be well, and all shall be well, and all manner of things shall be well." Julian responds to these words of divine assurance by reflecting on deeds that are done in the world and wrongs that are suffered in our lives that seem so evil that to conceive of good coming out of them is unimaginable. "I thought it impossible," she writes, "that all manner of things should be well."[17] How can the deep agonies of our world be transformed? How can the broken-ness within us be healed? And in particular Julian asks about "a certain person" in her life.[18] She wants to know if this one whom she especially loves will be well. Will all things be well for this one?

We do not know who this "certain person" in Julian's life was. She does not name her. Was she Julian's daughter, mother, lover, friend? We do not know. But Julian's question is essential. It is essential because it is a question of love. It is as important to speak of this one as it is to speak of the whole world. Because this is the language of love. Love speaks in particulars. It is the certain ones whom God has given us in our lives who have taught us to love and who have taught us what it is to love. When Julian asks about this "certain person" whom she loves, the answer she receives is "All shall be well." All will be well, and this one will be well. This one will be well, and all will be well. Our wellness belongs inseparably together.

Who are these ones whom we particularly love? Our child, our lover, our parent, our friend? And what are the brokennesses in their lives that we feel deeply—brokennesses that we may not even be able to imagine being made well? "I thought it impossible," says Julian, "that all manner of things should be well." It is important to express the disbelief that is within us and to ask again and again about these particular ones. What about them? How can all things possibly be made well for them? And we need to keep remembering that the preciousness of these ones who are special to us is the preciousness of special ones in other families, in other countries, in other species. We need to keep remembering that our wellness belongs inextricably together. To stay in touch with brokenness—whether that be in the hidden places of our own soul or in the intimacy of our family lives or the interrelatedness of our family's journey with the life of every family and every nation—is essential in the journey toward wholeness.

A few years after the Oklahoma City bombing, I received an invitation to speak at St. Paul's Cathedral in Oklahoma, just a block away from the bomb site. I learned that when the Murrah Federal Building blew up on the morning of

April 19, 1995, there were people praying in the cathedral
at the time. For a split second they saw above them blue sky.
Such was the implosion effect of the bombing that the roof
opened before collapsing back in on itself. It did not entirely
give way, but much structural damage was done, including
damage to a cross on top of the cathedral. It was a Celtic
cross with the traditional combination of cross and circle
overlapping. In the Celtic world, this had been used to point
to the oneness of the mystery of Christ and the mystery of
creation. The cross and the circle share the same center.
Christ and creation both come forth from the heart of
God. The deeper we move in the mystery of creation, the
closer we come to the Presence that Christ embodies.
The deeper we move in the mystery of Christ, the closer we
come to the heart of creation.

The Celtic cross on the top of St. Paul's Cathedral lost
one of its arms and part of its circle during the bomb blast.
What was most significant to me in hearing this story was
to learn that the cathedral congregation decided to retain
the broken cross as the symbol of their community. They
chose not to try to put all the pieces back together again.
Rather they chose not to forget, not to try to smooth over
the suffering of their people. The broken cross, now embed-
ded in a wall of the cathedral, continues to speak of the
brokenness of heart in Oklahoma City even after years of
rebuilding. It refuses to forget the 168 individuals lost even
as the stricken families have worked to rebuild their lives.
And it speaks powerfully of the brokenness that is everywhere present, of the parts within us and between us as
individuals and as nations that have been blasted apart by

confusions and falseness and suffering. St. Paul's Cathedral chose, as it sought new beginnings for Oklahoma City, to remain in touch with the agony. In doing so, it was a balm for the city's wounds.

In the sixth century on Iona, one of the rules that St. Columba gave to his monastic community was to pray "until thy tears come."[19] When tears flow, something very deep within us is stirring. Prayer is about getting in touch with the deepest dimension of our being. It is "the moistness of the soul," says Hildegard of Bingen, that leads us "to shed tears."[20] Jung speaks of the salt sea of our beginnings, the chaotic deep or the *prima materia* from which all life has come.[21] The saltiness of our tears comes from that place. They flow from the sea of our origins. They reconnect us to the moistness from which all life has arisen. And when we see through tears, we see differently. We see the world as if washed by a sea rain. When we weep for those we love, we see something of their diamond essence glistening forth. And when we weep, we see that the hard edges of life have become blurred. Even though brokenness may have caused our tears, when we weep we are close to life's oneness.

As a young man, I visited Dublin in Ireland for a number of days. I loved its streets and the River Liffey that runs through the heart of the city. I was alone and spent much of my time walking. One evening I wandered past St. Patrick's Cathedral and noticed that a performance of Handel's *Messiah* was about to begin. St. Patrick's choir had in fact been the first to sing Handel's new oratorio in 1742. I bought a ticket and entered. The overture was already under way. The cathedral was crowded, and the only place I could find a seat was halfway along a row very close to the front. I squeezed past some elegantly dressed couples in my old rain-soaked coat and sat down. Then came the words of the opening recitative, "Comfort ye, comfort ye My people." And I began to weep. Tears streamed down my face.

I still do not fully understand why as a young man, not much given to weeping, I cried in St. Patrick's Cathedral that evening. Yes, the tenor's voice was truly beautiful. And yes, the aesthetic of the cathedral was perfect, candlelit and warm on a cold, dark evening in Dublin. But it was more than that. I have often wondered if the tears were related to what I had been doing that day in Dublin, visiting O'Connell Street, where in July 1922 the Irish Civil War began. It was the same month that my father was born. And the rupture of a nation was breathed in by him and by his militant Protestant family in Northern Ireland in ways that have complicated his life's journey and the psyche of a whole people. Something of that division of soul I knew as a boy growing up in a family of Irish descent in Canada.

But I do not really know why I wept. All I really know is that when I heard the words "Comfort ye, comfort ye," my tears flowed. And when the tenor went on to sing of our "warfare . . . accomplished," our "iniquity . . . pardoned," I felt as if I were being addressed from the heart of life. The reality is that our "warfare" as an Irish people is not over, even though in the last number of years there has been transformation that previously we could not have imagined. The reality is that our "iniquity" of hatred and division continues in pockets of Irish society, even though the groundswell of refusal to participate in violence has been strong. But my experience that night in hearing the opening words of Handel's *Messiah* was of a balm for my woundedness, whether that be the woundedness I carry within myself as the son of an Irish Protestant or the deep wound of the human condition that we all carry within us. What is it that a balm for our wounds does?

During my four years at the abbey on Iona, I had personal contact with the Corrymeela Community in Northern Ireland. Since the mid-1960s, they have been a community of Protestants and Roman Catholics working for reconciliation in the Irish context. Quietly, and often behind the scenes, they prepared the groundwork for peace, whether through shared education programs in which both Protestants and Roman Catholics could participate, or through sanctuary movements in which young men from paramilitary organizations could find support and shelter for opting out of the cycle of violence. It was decades of such painstaking work by groups like Corrymeela that gradually transformed the situation on the ground in some of the most divided communities of Northern Ireland. And it was especially mothers, some of whom had experienced the deaths of their sons, who began to say a powerful "No" to the way of violence.

During a visit to the Corrymeela Community in the late 1980s, I remember making a cheap joke at the expense of Ian Paisley, the well-known Protestant extremist and belligerent political opponent of a united Ireland. No one laughed at my joke. They had no intention of being a balm for only one part of wounded Northern Ireland. They were committed to being a healing presence for both sides of the divide, a balm for all wounds. And part of their work of reconciliation was to stay faithfully in relationship with both sides of the woundedness. It was such commitment by Corrymeela and other groups that laid the groundwork for change. It was their vision and the detail of their lives and relationships that helped prepare the way for the Good Friday Peace Agreement in 1998, to which Ian Paisley was a signatory. It was the most significant political agreement for peace since the O'Connell Street riots in 1922. "Comfort ye, comfort ye, My people."

Jung says that "only the wounded physician heals."[22] Only to the extent that we are in touch with our own brokenness, both individually and collectively, will we be a strong presence of healing for others. Only to the extent that we know that the wounds we treat in others are part of our own woundedness will we experience the oneness of healing. Only to the extent that we remember that what we do to others is what we do to ourselves will we together be well again.

We lived in Canada for most of the 1980s, and in the mideighties there was a flood of Central American refugees across the American border into Canada. Some of them were simply seeking a better economic way of life. But many were political refugees, having fled their homelands to escape what at that time were the oppressive governments of El Salvador, Honduras, and Guatemala. Ali and I were working at McMaster University and created a space in our Chaplaincy Center to receive refugees and to help settle them in the Hamilton area.

Among the first families to arrive was Nora Melara-Lopez and her children. Nora was a high-spirited and high-heeled Latin American woman in her midthirties. She had been forced to flee Honduras with her three young children after the disappearance of her husband, José Eduardo Lopez, who had been working for human rights in his home country, courageously documenting the plight of the disappeared.[23] After Eduardo himself disappeared at the hands of a government death squad, Nora went public in Honduras, offering interviews to the media in the hope of finding her husband. She soon became an irritant to the government, and one night as she crossed the street in front of her home with her children, a car tried to run her down. She realized immediately that it was time to flee.

When we first met Nora in Canada, she still hoped that Eduardo might be found alive. She spoke of her last moment with him on a bus in Tegucigalpa. It was Christmas Eve, and she remembered him looking pale as he got off the bus. Later she wondered if he had a premonition of what lay ahead. She never saw him again. It had not been an easy relationship, her love affair with Eduardo. She had been a middle-class apolitical Baptist. He was an irreligious political advocate of the poor. With great laughter she recounted how Eduardo had persuaded her to move to a slum in the city. For a long time she refused, on the grounds that there was no plumbing in the area. Nora and Eduardo eventually divorced over their many disagreements. But when they got back together and remarried, Eduardo promised that if she would move to the slum with him, he would make sure there was running water and a flush toilet for their home. He did. The problem was that no other house in the slum had running water. So Nora's flush toilet became known as Nora's throne!

Christmas Eve 1984 was not the first time that Eduardo had been picked up by armed members of the National Directorate for Investigations. They had tried to intimidate him in 1981 by beating him up and severely torturing him. Afterwards as he lay on their bed at home and Nora tried to sooth with ointment the open wounds on his back, she cried, "I hate them. I hate them." And the irreligious Eduardo replied to his Christian wife, "Don't hate them. Forgive them. They don't know what they're doing."

It was Eduardo's disappearance that radicalized Nora. Until then she had been perplexed by his passion for the poor and frustrated by his willingness to endanger himself for the sake of others. But his disappearance changed that. There had been a woman who begged on the street corner near Nora's work. Nora had been passing her every day for months without really noticing her. Now she noticed. Her life had been caught up with getting ahead financially. Now she knew that her nation's wound was her wound.

Soon after Nora arrived in Canada, the flood of refugees was such that there needed to be a more organized reception and network of support. The Ecumenical Support Committee for Refugees was created, and Nora was appointed as the coordinator. To begin with, she shared office space in our Chaplaincy Center. One day as she interviewed an economic refugee from her home country, she learned that the man she was interviewing had been involved with the National Directorate of Investigations in Honduras. It was such a man who would have been part of the death squad that killed Eduardo. Nora excused herself from the interview, walked into Ali's office next door, and wailed. But this would not put her off receiving refugees from different political persuasions. She would try to be a balm for her nation's wounds. And part of what this meant for Nora in the years to come was a passionate and continued call that those responsible for wrong in her own country be brought to justice. "Eduardo's story," as she said at the Amnesty International trial in 2001, "needs to be heard and never forgotten."[24]

By the summer of 1943, Etty was no longer allowed to come and go from Westerbork. She was now a prisoner. "The misery here is quite terrible," she wrote, "and yet . . . against every new outrage and every fresh horror, we shall put up one more piece of love and goodness, drawing strength from within ourselves."[25] All along, Etty had a sense within herself of helping build a new day for the world. "And there is only one way of preparing for the new age," she said, "by living it even now in our hearts."[26] It was not just a matter of surviving physically. It was a matter of surviving without bitterness of soul and without hatred. Only thus, she believed, could she help prepare the new day. "The beat of my heart has grown deeper, more active, and yet more peaceful," she wrote during her last month in the camp, "and it is as if I were all the time storing up inner riches."[27]

On September 7, 1943, after a deportation order had been issued, Etty and her family boarded the transport of crowded freight cars bound for Poland. Before they crossed the Dutch border, Etty threw a postcard out of the train. It was found by farmers in a field and later sent to her friend Christine van Nooten in Amsterdam. It read, "We left the camp singing."[28] They reached Auschwitz on September 10. That same day, her mother and father were gassed, and Etty died on November 30, 1943. Only months earlier she had written, "If we should survive . . . without bitterness and without hatred, then we shall have a right to a say after the war. Maybe I am an ambitious woman: I would like to have just a tiny bit of a say."[29]

PART THREE

THE NEW HARMONY

CHAPTER 7

A PEARL OF
GREAT PRICE

During our years at the abbey on Iona, I received many requests from couples around the world wanting to be married on the holy island. My standard response was to invite them to come and speak with me about it. This was a tall order. Iona is a long way even from the Scottish mainland, so not many couples followed up their initial request. But John and Fran did. And when they met with me, they explained that their families were not supportive of their relationship. John was Roman Catholic and Fran was Protestant. The tragic division that has marked Northern Ireland and so many other parts of the Christian household was playing itself out between their families. John and Fran sensed that at the abbey they would find a place of welcome. I agreed to marry them in three month's time. The plan was that they would return to the abbey as guests for a week, and at the end of the week, in the midst of the Friday evening communion service, we would celebrate their marriage. And the abbey community would be their family of support.

By the end of that week three months later, John and Fran had been taken into the hearts of staff and guests alike. Older women poured affection and advice on Fran. Younger men were queuing up to be John's best man. The abbey kitchen baked a cake. And bottles of wine were appearing from every nook and cranny. Hundreds of us entered the abbey church that evening. The long table, an ancient Scottish practice, had been prepared. It stretched with candlelight the entire length of the chancel. The bread and wine were ready. We sat in concentric rows around the table with John and Fran at the center. It was like the great wedding feast imagined by St. John the Divine in his Book of Revelation, in which the union of heaven and earth is celebrated.

The word communion means "one with." It is of Latin origin, a combination of the word cum, meaning "with," and unus, meaning "one." But for a Latin speaker there would have been a rich image associated with it. Unus means "one" but unio means "a great pearl." The value of a great pearl is its oneness. A single unio is of much greater value than a collection of margaritae ("smaller pearls"). When we enter communion with another, we enter a precious unity. It is like the "pearl of great price" that Jesus uses to speak of the treasure of God (Matthew 13:46).

In the abbey that night, we witnessed a pearl of great price being formed. In giving themselves to each other in love, John and Fran were making a unio. And their oneness did not represent a loss of individuality. Quite the opposite. John and Fran were entering a union that was based on a deep cherishing of their distinctness as individuals. John at the table that night, with a beaming smile that even his heavy moustache did not hide, looked more himself than ever. Fran, with her shining eyes of certainty, looked more beautifully like Fran than she had ever done. And the rest of us too were caught up in transformation. We too were celebrating oneness. This, says Teilhard de Chardin, is the great gift of Christianity, "to be united while remaining oneself."[1] Communion is not about absorption or loss of self. It is about finding ourselves in one another.

At the end of the service, I invited everyone up to the refectory to continue the celebrations. As food and wine began to flow from the abbey kitchen, I was standing with John and Fran. Someone whom we did not recognize approached us with the wedding cake on a tray. When I introduced myself to him, the stranger replied, "I arrived on the island two hours ago and came to the service. You invited us all up to the reception. Perhaps I shouldn't be doing this, but when I entered the refectory I saw the cake and thought someone should be handing it out." It felt as if the *unio* of God had arrived. Everyone felt welcomed. Everyone had a part to play. And no one in particular was organizing it. John and Fran's marriage union was blessing a whole community with oneness.

This year I have experienced the weddings of both of my daughters, Kirsten's in India and Rowan's in Scotland. I was the priest at the liturgies. And despite my tears, or maybe because of my tears, I was able to see more clearly just how beautiful the marriage service is. There are variations of this in every tradition—whether Hindu or Muslim or Jewish—but in the Christian ceremony we hear the almost unbelievable words, "All that I am I give to you. And all that I have I share with you." Is this not a truly remarkable vow? A young woman and a young man standing in our midst and giving themselves wholly to each other. Two people forming a oneness. And two people's oneness blessing a whole community.

I shall always remember a particular premarriage counseling session at McMaster University in Canada where I was chaplain in the 1980s. I was discussing the marriage vows with a young couple, and especially the words, "All that I am I give to you. All that I have I share with you." At the end of my remarks, the young man responded, "But I can't say these words. I have a lot of money!" I admired his honesty, but had to say to him that if he was not prepared to take these vows, I was not prepared to preside at the wedding. There followed a number of forthright premarriage sessions before the young man agreed. It was an important moment in their relationship. These are truly remarkable words. And they point us to the costly essence of oneness.

What are the sacred communions into which we are being invited in the relationships of our lives and families? And what are the great communions into which we are being invited as a world today—the communion of the earth, the communion of nations, the communion of humanity's spiritual traditions? And what is the cost of this oneness?

Jesus teaches that we will truly find ourselves only by giving ourselves away in love. He says that discovering the oneness of God is like finding treasure hidden in a field.

Upon finding it, we want to sell everything we have in order to buy the field. Is this happening in our lives? Is it happening in the most important relationships of the world? If not, is it because we have yet to discover the treasure? Or is it because we are unwilling to pay the price? Have we glimpsed the hidden gold of oneness in our relationships yet been dissuaded by our individual ego, or by the ego of our nation or species, from truly giving ourselves? Carl Jung says that the "ego seizes the reins of power to its own destruction."[2] The extent to which we have served our sep-arateness rather than our oneness is the extent to which we have been deluded about what makes for true well-being. How are we to translate *cum-unus* into the relationships of our lives, both individually and collectively? How are we to reclaim Jesus' wisdom of truly finding ourselves by dying to our ego?

One of the great teachers in my life continues to be my younger son. Even though Cameron is well into his adoles-cence, he still speaks to me with a beautifully open heart. Some time ago at breakfast, we were having a conversation that touched upon spiritual wisdom. Halfway through our discussion, he said to me, quite candidly, "No offense to Jesus, Dad, but I don't think about him very much." I thought, what a beautiful boy is this that he is able to speak so transparently. I also realized that if I had tried saying such a thing at the breakfast table as a boy, I would probably have received a good swat across the head.

"No offense to Jesus, but I don't think about him very much." These words led to an interesting exchange with Cameron. I found myself saying to him that this was the greatness of Jesus, that he did not think about himself very much and that he would not be offended by Cameron's not thinking about him very much. This was Jesus' wisdom. He showed us that we truly find ourselves by losing our egocentricity. He showed us that true strength is to be found by loving the other as one's self. I also suggested to Cameron that if Jesus had thought about himself a great deal, we would probably have forgotten him long ago. "It is a good thing to think about Jesus," I said, "but not because Jesus needs us to be thinking about him. It is because Jesus shows us the way of love." He leads us to the pearl of great price.

How do we reclaim the wisdom of Jesus in the Christian household today and in our world of relationships? For many of us it has been a difficult journey. Rightly we have been appalled at the way in which Jesus has been hijacked by triumphalist religion. The truly humble one at the heart of our tradition has been used to prop up an often arrogant and irrelevant religious system. The son of compassion has been used to justify intolerance and even violence. Consequently many of us have gone silent about our great treasure. We have been so determined to distance ourselves from the misrepresentations of Jesus that we have failed to articulate the true essence of Jesus. When E. Stanley Jones, the twentieth-century American theologian who with Mahatma Gandhi helped lead the way in Indian interfaith relationship, was asked what the uniqueness of Christianity was, he said that Christianity's uniqueness was Jesus. This, of course, is the obvious answer. But maybe, under our many layers of doctrinal statements about Jesus, we have ended up missing the obvious. And we have ended up missing our greatest treasure.

An American rabbi was once asked what he thought of the words attributed to Jesus in St. John's Gospel, "I am the way, and the truth, and the life. No one comes to the Father except through me" (John 14:6). The rabbi replied, "Oh, I agree with these words." To which the surprised questioner asked further, "But how can you as a rabbi believe that Jesus is the way, the truth, and the life?" "Because," answered the rabbi, "I believe that Jesus' way is the way of love, that Jesus' truth is the truth of love, and that Jesus' life is the life of love. No one comes to the Father but through love."

The subtext in how Christianity has often interpreted these words is, "*We* are the way, the truth, and the life. No one comes to the Father but through *us*. No one comes to God except through our beliefs, our sacraments, our apostolic succession." But whether it is an exclusivizing of Jesus or an idolizing of our particular beliefs about him, the result is the same. We miss the rabbi's point, that the only way to God is through love. Instead of seeing Jesus as embodying the way of love that we are to follow, the truth of love that we are to believe, and the life of love that we are to live, we have turned his teachings into a set of propositional truths about Jesus. We have pretended that the most important thing is to give assent to particular beliefs rather than to follow the way of love, the truth of love, and the life of love. And part of what we have ended up doing is creating a Jesus who is so insecure that he needs us to be thinking about him all the time.

The danger has been to take our eyes off the imperative of love. The danger has been to think that we can have the pearl without paying the price, that we can have peace in our relationships without giving our hearts to one another, that we can enjoy oneness with creation without living a costly communion with the earth and its species. Teilhard de Chardin says that the universe will be "unified only through personal relations."[3] It will become one only under the influence of love. Teilhard calls this the "amorization" of the universe, the healing of the world by loving.[4] Only love has the capacity to transform the individual parts of our lives and world into a living cum-unus. Nothing else can do it. All the mightiest weapons of the world put together do not have the power to change a single heart. They have never been able to do it, and they will never be able to do it. So why do we depend so heavily on force to the neglect of personal relations? Why do we pretend that we can be secure as nations, as communities, and as individuals without love's costly commitments? "Love," says Teilhard, "is the most universal, the most tremendous and the most mysterious of the cosmic forces." How much truth and energy are we losing, he asks, by neglecting our "incredible power to love"?[5]

When I studied theology at the University of Edinburgh, there was a monk named Roland Walls, whose countenance was the Christian equivalent of the Dalai Lama's. And like the Dalai Lama he would laugh. And he would get us laughing at ourselves and at the absurdity of some of our religious claims. His great gift was to combine the heart and the head, the intellect and prayer. I first encountered him when he was teaching at New College in Edinburgh. I arrived late for class that morning and was surprised to find a man teaching us who looked as though he had come from the local homeless shelter. His clothes were a bit tatty. And he seemed less than immaculately groomed and presented.

When I entered, Roland was standing at the front of the class half-turned toward us. His attention was on an icon, a copy of Rublev's Trinity, which he had perched on a chair that was sitting on top of his desk. Roland was addressing us, but the focus of his attention was the icon, explicating its main themes and images. Gradually, without our really noticing the transition, he moved from addressing us to addressing the icon. And before we knew it, the lecture had become prayer. We were drawn into an experience of communion in which the icon was like a window into the divine Presence.

Roland lived at the Community of the Transfiguration in Roslin, just outside Edinburgh. It was a small and very simple religious community. Each of the brothers lived in a garden hut, and their chapel consisted of two garden huts joined together. They also had a little house in which to eat together and receive guests. One never knew who would be gathered around the meal table at Roslin. On one side of you there might be a bishop, Oxford educated and aristocratic sounding. On the other side, a convict who had just been released from prison, hard edged and rough spoken. The conversation would range from theological matters to broad political debate and the simplest sharing of stories, peppered again and again by Roland's laughter and by his simple reiteration of the wisdom of Jesus, the way of compassion.

Roland told us the story of the beginnings of their community. He and his brothers went on a preparatory retreat to a more established monastery nearby, the Trappist community of Nunraw in the Scottish Borders. It was a three-day preparation in which a wise old monk would guide them into the essentials of community life together. On the first day, the old monk shuffled into the room, sat down, and said to them, "Today I have just one thing to say to you. 'God loves you.' Now go away and think about that." So off they went in their discipline of silence for the day, walking the monastic gardens and reflecting in their individual cells on the great mystery of God's love for us.

On the second morning, the old monk again shuffled into the room, sat down, and said, "Today I have just one thing to say to you. 'You can love God.' Now go away and think about that." So off they wandered for their second day of silence, pondering the great truth that God not only loves us but also longs for our love. Not only are we the recipients of love. We are the beloved partners in an eternal love affair.

On the third morning, Roland wondered what could possibly be added to the essential teachings of the first two days. God loves us, and we can love God. Was there anything to add to this completeness? The old monk again shuffled into the room, sat down, and said to them, "Today I have just one thing to say to you. 'You are to love one another.' Now go away and live this truth as a community." The pearl of great price, living together in love.

Jesus said, "Do to others as you would have them do to you" (Matthew 7:12). Like never before in the history of humanity, we are becoming aware that what we do to others is what we do to ourselves. And not only what we do to others as human beings but what we do to others as species, what we do to the earth and its elements, what we do to the rivers and to our skies. The way we treat the cosmos is the way we treat ourselves. Thomas Berry, applying the Jewish theologian Martin Buber's insight into the nature of true relationship, says that the world has become an "it" to us, a mere object for our use and abuse, rather than a "Thou," a sacred partner in relationship.[6] What we are being invited into, says Richard Tarnas, is a "genuine dialogue" with the universe, a communion in which we learn to treat the other, every other, as "Thou."[7]

Meister Eckhart says that the one "who truly loves can only love one thing."[8] True love is not divided in its loyalties and energies. To love God, to love oneself, and to love one's neighbor, as Jesus teaches, is impossible unless they are one. The one cannot occur without the other. To truly love one's family is to love the essence of every family. To truly love one's nation is to enter a "genuine dialogue" with the heart of every nation. To truly love God is to look for the sacred in everything that has being.

Last year, I spent a day hiking through Glen Tromie in the Cairngorm Mountains of Scotland. It was midwinter, and the ground was covered by a thick layer of snow. I had walked for hours without meeting anyone. I love the

intimacy of this glen. Some of its neighbors, like Glen Feshie
and Glen Einich, are wilder and grander, but Glen Tromie
is a perfect winter walk with its smaller proportions and
shelter of hills on either side. During the hike, I realized
just how much I love this land. I also wondered how it
is that I hold this love together with my love for other
landscapes, other wildnesses. I thought of the vast stretches
of sky and sandstone mesas in the high desert of New
Mexico or the ancient rock formations and lakes of the
Canadian Shield where I spent my summers as a boy.
What is it that allows the love of these different places to
be one?

At the same time, my thoughts turned to the particulari-
ties of our lives and relationships. How do we remain true
in our family life, in our devotion to nation, in our loyalty
to religious tradition, and at the same time be in faithful
relationship with those beyond the boundaries of these
defined relationships? Can we live a conciliation between
the two? I had been reading Jung's thoughts about what he
calls the "transcendent function."[9] It is a way of uniting
supposed opposites. It is a disciplined practice of placing
oneself in between two worlds, or at the midpoint between
two extremes that seem irreconcilable, and faithfully waiting
until the intersecting of their shared essence occurs. It is a
way of seeking oneness between the two ends of a spectrum
that otherwise fall into duality.

What are the dualisms of our lives? I love this place and
not that place. I love my family, my nation, my religious
inheritance, my species but not those people, those traditions, those species, those life-forms. And what about the

ultimate dualisms that Jesus addresses in his teachings? I love God but not my brother. Or I love myself but not my neighbor. Jesus transcends these separations by disclosing the oneness of love. The one "who truly loves," says Eckhart, "can only love one thing." So radical is this oneness that it means that what we do to ourselves is what we do to God. What we do to our neighbor, what we do to the earth, is what we do to ourselves.

As I walked through Glen Tromie reflecting on my love of one place in relation to my love of other places, I was searching for a "transcendent function," something that would hold them together. And what emerged in my thoughts was the medieval concept of *anima mundi*, or "the soul of the earth." The Scottish landscape in which I was walking can seem so entirely different from the New Mexican landscape. One is eternally moist and verdant. The other is a high desert of sand with occasional outrageous outbursts of color and blossom. And yet in both places I breathe deeply. I inhale the soul of creation in these landscapes and am alive to its oneness. It is what Teilhard de Chardin calls the "fragrance" of the Feminine deep within the body of the earth, that quality within matter that awakens our desire for union.[10] But the modern world, especially since the seventeenth century, has lost its awareness of the *anima mundi*. Matter is no longer animated by spirit. Instead, says Richard Tarnas, the universe is viewed as a "soulless vacuum."[11] And humanity is regarded as an exception to the rest of the cosmos instead of as an expression of the cosmos. Spiritual and psychological qualities are located exclusively in the human psyche rather than in the vastness of the universe and in everything that has being. We have raised humanity into a separate category from the earth instead of seeing that we carry within ourselves the essence of the earth.

Toward the end of my day in Glen Tromie, I was reveling in a sense of the *anima mundi* all around me. The whiteness of the landscape, the soft curves of the mountain peaks, the flow of the river were like a living body infused with soul. By now it was twilight as I headed out of the glen. But suddenly ahead of me on the path was a pack of dogs. They had picked up my scent and were rushing at me full speed and angry. No one was with them. They came from the direction of the hunting lodge and kennels nearby. Clearly they had been pent up for too long and were now exploding with aggressive energy.

All my attention was focused on the big hounds at the front of the pack. I thought if I could speak to them, calling out firmly but unthreateningly, I could establish a type of relationship with them and settle them. They stopped about ten feet in front of me, still barking furiously but by now unsure what to do. Although part of me was frightened, I felt a calmness in my voice. Years of experience growing up as a boy with dogs, and the fact that the big hounds had now stopped and were listening to me, made me think I was going to be all right.

Out of the corner of my eye, I was aware of a little dog that I assumed to be a puppy. So he was of no concern to me. My focus remained on the big hounds directly in front of me. But suddenly the little dog bit me from the backside. It was not a puppy after all. It was a small terrier. He dug his teeth into the back of my leg, cutting my skin and drawing blood. It lasted but a split second and then he was gone, rejoining the others. The pack now began to disperse a little, enough at least to let me move forward. But now as I hobbled on, limping slightly at the sharp sting of the bite, I kept my eyes on the terrier as well. And soon I was safely away.

An experience of *anima mundi*! Never an experience to be romanticized. There are always little terriers in life that will bite our backside if we are not careful. We need to give our attention to them as well, our concentrated attention. This is not to detract from the reality of my experience of elation in the glen—even though I will never again hike Glen Tromie without a walking stick in hand! I do not doubt that there is an *anima* or spiritual dimension within everything that has being, and that within each life-form is the Soul from whom we and all things come. I do believe, however, that we have to learn how to be in relationship with all things again, how to approach one another, and how to reassure each other. And we need to know the risks. We need to be aware of how fragmented the unity is and just how deeply our wholeness has been divided by fears and aggressions that have further compounded the brokenness. We need to find ways of giving real attention to one another, of entering into "genuine dialogue" with the earth and its creatures. And in all of this we need to believe again in our "incredible power to love." It is deep within us. It is deep within everything that has being. And it alone holds the strength to redeem our relationships.

Perhaps the profoundest words ever uttered were "God is love" (1 John 4:16). They are attributed to John the Beloved, the one who leaned against Jesus at the Last Supper and was said to have heard the heartbeat of God. The profoundest utterances in life are always the simplest of utterances. The problem with truth is not that it is too complicated for expression. The problem with truth is that it is too simple for expression. Three simple words, "God is love," which is to say that when we love, we are one with God. And when we do not love, we are not one with God.

According to legend, John the Beloved lived to a ripe old age, until over a hundred. He was the cousin of Jesus, son of Mary's sister, Salome. Youngest among the disciples, he had been especially loved. After the crucifixion, he was silent for years amidst the uncertainties and violence of Jerusalem. With the destruction of the Temple, he fled Palestine for Ephesus with Mary the Mother. There he discovered his voice again and denounced the inhumanities of empire. He was sent into political exile for years on the island of Patmos, and finally as an old man returned to Ephesus. This is the fascinating stuff of legend. How much of it actually occurred we do not know. What is certain, however, is that the Community of John believed in love. "God is love," they said, "and those who live in love live in God, and God lives in them" (1 John 4:16).

One of the last stories of St. John's life relates to his being so weak that he had to be carried to morning and evening prayer in Ephesus. And as he was being carried by members of his community, he would say just one thing to

them: "Little children, love one another."[12] After a while
they became frustrated by this. Here was the great man,
John the Beloved. He had grown up with Jesus. He had been
part of the inner circle of disciples who entered Jerusalem
amidst the song and jubilation of crowds who hoped this
would be a new era in the life of their nation. He had witnessed the crucifixion. He had become like a son to Mary.
He had dreamed of a new heaven and a new earth. He had
threatened the empire with the power of his words and paid
the price with years of exile. There was so much he could
tell them. But all he would say was "Little children, love one
another." Finally, one day on the way to prayer they asked
him, "Teacher, why do you always say this?" To which John
replied, "Because it was the Lord's precept, and if it alone
is done, it is enough."[13]

Do we need something more than this wisdom? Or is
it just that we pretend we need more and end up doing less?
We so much think we need to do more than love our enemy
that we end up downplaying our greatest strength, our
"incredible power to love." We so much think we need to
focus primarily on our defensive strategies, our accumula-
tion of more and more wealth, our obsession with the
human species to the neglect of other species, that we end
up ignoring our greatest capacity to redeem the relationships of our lives and world, by loving one another.

John and Fran believed in the power of love even though
their families did not support them. In one another they
had found love's pearl of great price and were prepared to
let everything else go. If love alone is followed, says St. John,
"it is enough." A number of years after their Iona wedding,

they gave birth to their first child, Uist, a beautiful boy. They asked my Ali to baptize him in the River Isla. It was a cold day as we clambered down to the river and found a place midstream that was stable enough for Ali and the little holy family to stand. And gathered together on the riverbank with tears of delight were the two families, one Roman Catholic and one Protestant. Uist's birth had brought them together.

Uist's birth was the symbol of a new beginning. The word *symbol* comes from the Greek *sum*, meaning "together," and *bolos*, meaning "throw." A symbol throws together or brings into relationship what has previously been unconnected. The birth was a union of opposites, of male and female but also of Roman Catholic and Protestant. Uist was of John, and he was also of Fran. Yet he was his own person, entirely unique. As Jung says in his work on symbols, the thing that is born of a marriage of opposites is "not a compromise but something new."[14] Uist was not the dilution of a Roman Catholic family or the diminution of a Protestant family. He was a new creation. And his life was not bound by the limitations of his heritage.

The divine child born as a symbol of unity is an image cherished in many traditions. And it appears at the very heart of our Christian household. The Christ-child is born of heaven and earth, of God and humanity, of time and eternity. He is not simply one or the other. He is both. And he shows us that we are both, that the spiritual and the material are one, that heaven and earth intersect in us. In the ancient prayers of the Hebrides in Scotland, the Christ-child is referred to as "Son of the sun" and "Son of the moon."[15]

He brings together what has been considered opposite. He is the marriage of spirit and matter, the seen and the unseen, grace and nature. As Teilhard de Chardin says, he is the synthesis of what we "could never have dared join together."[16] He is the symbol of oneness. He shows us the pearl of great price. It is ours if we will have it. But it will cost us everything. Because its cost is love.

CHAPTER 8

REDISCOVERING AN OLDER UNITY

The new harmony that we seek is not the construction of a new unity. It is, as Thomas Merton says, the rediscovery of an "older unity."[1] It is not the laying of a new foundation for relationship. It is the fresh uncovering of life's original groundwork. In the final weeks of his life, Thomas Merton, the American Trappist monk and visionary for peace, met in Asia with leaders of other religious traditions. One of the last things he said to them was, "My dear brothers, we are already one. But we imagine that we are not. What we have to recover is our original unity. What we have to be is what we are."[2]

Our experiences of communion in life are glimpses into this original unity. They are a rediscovery of what we most truly are—one. Whether it is our experience of gazing into the vast infinity of night skies or looking deep into the eyes of one we love, it is the recognizing of a oneness we did not create but have been gifted with. It is the rediscovery of a harmony that precedes us, the remembering of a unity that is deep in the body of the universe.

132

The best of our rituals and religious disciplines of communion reflect this. They do not create oneness. They help us remember our oneness. They do not make unity. They release our unity. They free us from the forgetfulness of thinking we are essentially separate. They liberate us from the delusions of isolated individuality. In our sacrament of communion in the Christian household, when we share one bread and one cup together, we recite Jesus' words, "Do this to remember me." We do this to re-member, to bring back into relationship again what has been forgotten, to reawaken within ourselves the way of oneness, the truth of oneness, the life of oneness.

One of the great blessings of my four years at the abbey on Iona was gathering together with people from around the world every Friday evening to share bread and wine at the long table. This ancient Scottish practice of communion, in which a table extends the entire length of the chancel, is celebrated weekly at the abbey. Gathered around the table were always many nations and languages, many colors and denominations. It was an experience of the world at table together. And when the world gathers together at table, there is always the sublime as well as the ridiculous.

I shall never forget one Friday evening in particular. Our service had begun at the east end of the cathedral. During the first hymn, I led the procession from the nave into the chancel so that we could be seated around the long table. The first to join me at the head of the table were some lads from Easterhouse, a rough council housing scheme in Glasgow. Perhaps they had never been in a church before.

Sometimes this was the case on Iona, when groups from different traditions and backgrounds gathered together.

The lads were wide-eyed about the proceedings and appeared happy enough to be there. But sitting at table together was probably not what they had expected. The combination of food and drink, together with their being warmly welcomed into the life of the community, made them feel so much at home that they pulled out their cigarettes and lit up at the table. I was hesitant to inhibit their style, but felt they should at least know that this was not our custom at the abbey. So as the rest of the congregation was still singing and making its way from the nave to the table, I had a quiet word with the boys, to which they obligingly responded by putting out their cigarettes. I thought the worst was over. In fact the comedy had just begun. When it came to sharing the bread and the wine, they were the first to receive. And by the time the chalice reached the fourth lad, it had been drained dry. The celebration of an older unity!

As well as absurd occasions at the abbey, there were truly extraordinary moments of oneness. There was the time when Zaki Badawi, a prominent scholar of the Islamic community in Britain, led us in a Muslim call to prayer in the abbey church. This was a sound that had never been heard within the eight-hundred-year-old walls of the abbey. And yet it sounded as if it deeply belonged. It was the sound of a new-ancient harmony that was being born again within us and between us.

And there was the week when Rabbi Jeremy Milgrom, the cofounder of Clergy for Peace in Jerusalem, taught Torah at the abbey. The agreement was that he would teach Scripture in the mornings and for the rest of the day join in as much of the community's life as he wished. Jeremy fully participated in the pattern of our days. Every morning he would join us for prayer in the abbey church. In the evenings he would sing hymns with us and listen to our Scriptures.

Toward the end of the week, we asked Jeremy if he would preach at the long-table celebration of communion. Being a good rabbi, he said he did not know a precedent of a Jewish rabbi preaching at a communion service. But he knew a precedent of a rabbi singing a table blessing at a Christian communion, so he would sing a table blessing for us. When it came time for the blessing, Jeremy gave it a ten-minute introduction. So we had a sermon after all!

Ali was presiding that evening, so she was seated at the head of the table. And because Jeremy was preaching—or giving the table blessing as he called it—he sat immediately next to her. We assumed he was simply wanting to be present for communion rather than to fully participate in communion. When it came time for the sharing of the bread and wine, however, Ali, intending simply to start the bread around the table, handed it to Jeremy so that he could then pass it on to his neighbor. But Jeremy received the bread and ate before serving his neighbor. And he did the same with the cup.

An older unity was being rediscovered among us, a oneness that precedes our divisions, a unity that underlies our differentiations. In speaking about the communion service later on that night, Rabbi Jeremy explained that it had not been his intention to receive the bread and wine when he came to the service. But as he sat at table he realized that it was all so deeply familiar, the sharing of bread and wine at table together. He also realized that he had been so welcomed as a Jewish rabbi into the abbey community that he could receive the bread and the wine according to his own tradition. He knew that he was not being untrue to us or to his own inheritance. He was being deeply true. He also knew that he wanted to be true to an older unity, the unity of the human soul, the unity of the earth.

Meister Eckhart in the fourteenth century said that "to be united . . . is to be one with God."[3] Elsewhere he puts it more emphatically when he says, "be one in order that you may find God."[4] Have we thought that we can find God in separation? Have we thought we can be complete without one another? As Thomas Berry says, "Nothing is itself without everything else. Nothing exists in isolation."[5] This is the growing realization at the heart of humanity's new consciousness. Will we choose to apply it as Jews and Christians and Muslims? And will we also choose to realize that until we apply it religiously, politically, and economically, there will be no peace on earth, and we will not be well within ourselves?

Eckhart says that "identity is unity."[6] Our truest self-understanding is based on the interrelatedness of all things. When will we cease to pretend that our identity can be found primarily in separation as Christians or Jews or Muslims or any other form of religious identification? These great religious traditions are secondary identities, as are our nations and cultures and races. They are given to serve our deepest identity, not to displace our deepest identity. "Be one in order that you may find God," says Eckhart. It is in our oneness that we will find true identity. It is in unity that we will find God.

What are the older unities we are being invited to rediscover in our lives and world? And what are the boundaries we are to cross for the sake of healing today, boundaries between our nations and religions that before have seemed so absolute? What is the new humility into which we are being called if we are to be truly strong in our relationships, both individually and collectively? And in all of this how do we cherish the distinct lines of definition that have been a blessing to us in our lives and traditions, without allowing them to be the separating lines that are destroying us?

My father was reared in a militant Protestant community in Northern Ireland, off the Shankhill Road in Belfast. Hatred for Roman Catholics and Irish Republicans ran deep in the blood. He was never directly involved in the violence, and he did not expressly voice it in his life, but the antipathies of his divided homeland infected his soul as a boy growing up. And never in his life had he been willing to visit the south of Ireland. The sin of division had been passed from one generation to the next.

A few years ago, however, as my father planned what he thought might be his last trip across the Atlantic from Canada, he asked that I make arrangements for us to have a family holiday in the south of Ireland. I found a cottage on the beautifully wild coastline of the Dingle Peninsula in County Kerry. On the first Sunday, we took my parents into the nearby town of Dingle Bay, naively thinking there might be a variety of churches to choose from. We could find only one, and it was not in my father's tradition. I began to feel anxious. Looking back on it now, I realize how ridiculous it was of me to try to protect my eighty-three-year-old father from having to enter a Roman Catholic church. I am deeply ecumenical in my convictions, so much so that for me it applies primarily to relations between different faiths, not simply between different Christian denominations. I have given years of my life to working for peace within the Christian household and between the great religions of humanity, in the belief that this is the true basis for peace in our world.

So it was absurd to find myself standing on the street outside St. Mary's Church in Dingle Bay saying to my father, "We don't have to go in there." To which he responded, "I want to go to church, and I want to go in there." But still unsure, I said, "But we don't have to stay for the entire service. We can leave after the liturgy of the word." To which my father replied, "I want to go to church, and I want to stay for the entire service."

The Roman Catholic priest was a delightful Irish blether. And I could tell that his warm style was endearing him to my father's heart. When it came to the intercessions, the priest said in his thick Irish accent, "Now we pray for the weather, Lord. It's not been too bad, but it could be much better. And we have people visiting from around the world, Lord, and we'd like them to see our beautiful country. So we pray for the weather, Lord." And on and on he chattered.

After the liturgy of the word, we moved into the mass proper. And when the invitation for communion came, there was my Irish Protestant father with tears streaming down his face moving forward to receive the bread and the wine from an Irish Roman Catholic priest. There is hope for the world. I was witnessing the rediscovery of an older unity. I was seeing the crossing of a boundary that before would have seemed unimaginable to a Belfast boy born off the Shankhill Road. Later that same day, my mother, who has always been a Scottish Presbyterian teetotaler, accompanied me to a Dingle pub for a celebration of live Irish folk music. Truly there is hope for the world!

How do we enable change? How do we together cross boundaries that in the past have seemed impenetrable? Teilhard de Chardin, early in the twentieth century, prophetically anticipated the awareness of earth's oneness that we are now in the midst of. "All living beings," he wrote from the trenches of the First World War, "are one being."[7] What we do to one another as nations, what we do to other species of the earth, is what we do to ourselves. Julian of Norwich in the fourteenth century said that God is the "ground" of all things. God is "nature's substance."[8] What we do to the earth, what we do to ourselves, is what we do to God. The twelfth-century teacher Hildegard of Bingen in her dreamlike awarenesses heard the divine words, "The human species . . . has its roots in me."[9] "All life lights up out of me."[10] The deeper we move in any created thing, the closer we come to what she calls the "radiance" of God.[11]

These Christian teachers have been saying the same thing over the centuries, that woven through the fabric of the universe is the being of God, and that if somehow we were to extract this "radiance" from the body of the universe, all things would cease to exist. It is not an extra feature of the cosmos. It is the soul of the cosmos. It is not an added dimension to the four elements of creation. It is the very essence of creation. It is, as Jung says, "the *quinta essentia*" that holds all things together.[12] It is the *quintus*, the fifth thing, that holds in harmony the four elements of earth, air, fire, and water that constitute the body of the universe. And for Jung the true quintessence of all things is "the *imago Dei*."[13] Wherever we look, into whichever blade of grass we gaze, into whichever part of the heavens we explore, into whichever human countenance we peer, there is the holy image. There is life's true essence.

These have been the insights to emerge again and again over the centuries from some of our greatest teachers. They have encouraged us to look for the sacred at the heart of everything and to know that that sacred essence is the unity of life. It is one thing to glimpse this essence, and even to believe that this quintessence is not simply a field of energy but a living presence. But it is another thing to shape our lives in relation to this holy essence and to be part of re-embodying oneness in the relationships of our world. How is harmony again to be born from within us? How is the original unity of life to be rediscovered in our lives and relationships?

Last year I had a dream in which an alchemist-like woman whom I did not know was summoning pieces of fish into a chrysalis-type structure, a place of transformation. The individual segments of fish seemed entirely unrelated to each other until they passed through the large cocoon-shaped chrysalis. But on the other side of the chrysalis, they emerged complete as a bright shining salmon, all of the pieces reconnected into a living whole. In the dream, I thought it was like the reverse of a meat grinder. The separate parts were now reunited and living. Toward the end of the dream, a word appeared visually in front of me, which upon waking I could not remember. But later in the morning it came back to me. The word was quintus.

There are many strands to this dream. One is the unknown woman who draws the parts back into a whole. She represents a feminine dimension within me, within us, which the dream suggests I am not yet fully conscious of. Her gift is to bring back into relationship what has been torn apart. Her charism is relational. And her wisdom is to know that the segments are part of a whole. In the dream, the pieces seem so fragmented, so separate, that it is easy to believe there is no connection. What is this grace of feminine, relational wisdom within us waiting to be reborn in our families and nations and among us as an earth community? And do we know that this gift is within us?

The chrysalis-type structure is another significant part of the dream. The word chrysalis comes from the Greek khrusos, which means "gold." It is used to refer to the transition state in the metamorphosis of an insect, especially from larva into butterfly. This is a hidden moment, the golden alchemical moment of transformation. And in the development of an insect, it is a quiescent time. Nothing appears to be happening in the stillness of the chrysalis. How do we enable one another to pay attention to the hidden gold of stillness within us where despite outward observation, the beginnings of transformation can be born? And how in our lives and relationships are we to recover faithful and trusting practices of stillness in order that deep change may emerge from the heart of our being?

The word that appears visually toward the end of the dream, when the bright, beautiful salmon appears, is *quintus*. It is Latin for "fifth." The salmon represents something that is quintessential to life, something more than the four elements of which its body is constituted. Known for giving its life in order to spawn new beginnings, the salmon discloses something of life's *quinta essentia*. It is like a window into the mystery of relationship at the heart of the universe. Life is not composed simply of its material elements. Its quintessence is the longing for relationship and for new beginnings.

Interestingly it was not a butterfly that emerged from the chrysalis in my dream. The butterfly also is a symbol of resurrection, which in the Christian tradition occurs when grace and nature combine, when grace awakens within our nature something that has been assumed dead and beyond hope. Instead what emerged from the chrysalis was a salmon. In the ancient Celtic world, the salmon was a symbol of wisdom, which in later Christian Celtic symbolism became associated with Christ, or more specifically with the wisdom of Christ's way, which is the way of love, the truth of love, and the life of love. This is the *quinta essentia* that holds all things together. Without love, the elements of our lives disperse. It is the *quintus*, the essential fifth, that brings all things into the wholeness of relationship. Love is the gold at the heart of life's chrysalis. And it is not simply gold at the heart of the human chrysalis. It is the desire for relationship at the heart of the universe.

Meister Eckhart says that "all creatures . . . seek the One."[14] This longing is deep within the stuff of our nature. It is deep within the body of the cosmos. We seek the One by seeking oneness with each other, by seeking to be in relationship with the rest of life, by living in relation to everything that has being. The tragedy of our reality is that we have fallen out of touch with this holy natural longing. Divisions that have multiplied divisions, and fears that have fed upon fears drive us further and further apart. Grace, says Teilhard de Chardin, is the "seed of resurrection" sown in our nature.[15] And the greatest of graces, love, is what reawakens the deep longings of our being, the hunger for oneness, the desire for unity. How do we bring this greatest of graces to the relationships of our lives—our relationship with the earth, our relationship as nations, our relationship as wisdom traditions?

Our oldest unity is our relationship with the earth. And yet this is the relationship that we have so deeply neglected. For many of earth's species, we are now too late to redeem the relationship. They are becoming extinct at an alarming and accelerating pace. We are in danger of a deep impoverishment of life as we have known it. But there is also hope for the community of earth. We are living in the midst of what Berry calls a "moment of grace."[16] As never before in the history of humanity, we are becoming aware of our interrelatedness. We are beginning to comprehend that what we do to other species is what we do to ourselves. We are beginning to perceive that what we do to other nations and peoples is what we do to our own soul. The question is whether we will choose to translate this emerging consciousness into transformative action. And the further question is where we will find strength and vision for this work.

In almost every area of life, humanity is being invited to turn its attention to reestablishing our original unity with the earth. This is true economically as more and more we realize that an economy based on disrespect for the earth is unsustainable. It is also true scientifically and educationally as we increasingly come to understand that every discipline of study is interrelated with every other discipline. And the study of ecology is at the center of this network of inter-relationship. We are realizing that without a knowledge of the earth and an awareness of its origins and unfolding history, every other field of study is impoverished. This is as true for psychology and the arts as it is for the traditional sciences. And it is equally true for theology and for our disciplines of prayer and religious practice. All of them need to relate to the essential oneness of the earth.

During our years in Portsmouth, my role in the Church of England was to develop St. John's House as a spirituality resource at the heart of Britain's most densely populated city. Ali and I instinctively knew that the neglected garden of the old vicarage on Copnor Road was going to play a significant part in the work. We set about hacking away at the thick undergrowth of briars and soon saw that there was a natural curve to the original planting of the garden, defined by some fine old trees, including a fig tree, a bay, and a copper beech. And we realized that this curved line of trees provided us with an outline of what the new shape and use of the garden could be. We saw that there could be a central circular pathway in between the house and the line of trees, bordered by lavender and covered by a pergola of wisteria. And off this central open space, with its cathedral-like expansiveness, there could be distinct garden areas like side chapels to the main garden sanctuary.

This is exactly what began to happen in the old vicarage garden. The central space with its circular pathway was created. And in one of the adjoining areas, we developed a contemplation space planted heavily in bamboo with Japanese meditation garden stones and motifs. In another there was an old baptismal font of beautifully carved granite, around which we planted traditional English shrubs and flowers. There was also an altar garden done in wild Scottish heathers and sylphlike birches. And finally there was a play area with a slide and swing for the children, and a vegetable patch in which to provide for the kitchen table.

The Anglican Diocese of Portsmouth caught the vision of this project and provided funding to enable it to happen. The diocese also provided me with the remaining pieces of white marble from the altar of St. John's Church, Portsea, that had been salvaged from the church after its destruction during a Second World War blitz on Portsmouth. With these fragments, and aware of the hundreds of people who had died during the blitz, I began to build a simple altar in the garden of St. John's House surrounded by a circle of marble flagstone slabs. And here we began to celebrate communion every week in the context of creation. As I fashioned this space with my hands, I became increasingly aware that what I was doing physically was what I was also attempting to do spiritually: taking the pieces of our inheritance to shape a new beginning in the context of creation.

This is what many of us are seeking today in the Christian household and in other spiritual traditions: to take precious fragments from the wreckage of what our religious traditions have often become and to create something new in the midst of humanity's growing earth awareness. Our attempts are sometimes muddled and uncertain because we are in uncharted territory. But they are also indicators of the way forward, providing us with clues as to what the human soul is searching for in its desire to rediscover our ancient unity with the earth.

Usually there were very few people at our weekly celebrations of communion. But there was a sense that what we were part of was something much bigger than we were, something much broader than our particular religious practice or specific spiritual tradition. We were part of a much vaster quest, to link the wisdom and disciplines of our inheritance to the growing consciousness of earth's oneness. We were a simple expression of a broadly diverse movement of the Spirit, to reconnect the human journey to the earth's journey.

Recently I learned that the Church of England had sold off St. John's House and that the garden had been destroyed to build a crowded collection of houses with virtually no green space between the buildings. Perhaps as a teacher I am naive to the financial demands of running a large religious organization. But as a religious tradition, we must not be naive to the imperative of staying in close relationship with the earth. Perhaps it will be argued that the money from the sale was used for good purposes, perhaps even to help relieve poverty in inner-city Portsmouth. But unless we also find ways of addressing the poverty of our liturgies and theology in relation to creation, we will become increasingly irrelevant to the human journey. This is not to focus criticism on one particular diocese. It is rather to say that this disconnect with creation has been a prevalent feature in much of our Western religious and cultural inheritance, and that if we continue on this path, we will contribute not to the rediscovery of an older unity but to the furtherance of greater and greater fragmentation.

Hildegard speaks of "Earth's greening power."[17] This literally is what we need to come back into relationship with, the life force deep within creation that allows it to green and to grow. But this greening power is also something we need to rediscover within ourselves and in the important relationships of our lives and world. It is the quintessence of our being and of the universe, the desire for life and new beginnings, the longing to be in fertile relationship with everything around us. It is this desire that led Rabbi Jeremy to cross boundaries and participate in the sharing of bread and wine at a Christian table of communion. It is this longing that surfaced from deep within my father's heart and prompted him to receive the bread and wine of unity from a Roman Catholic priest. It is this yearning that will guide us as a world into the rediscovery of our oneness.

A few years ago, we as a family celebrated Easter at a little Episcopal church in Edinburgh. When it came time to receive communion, we found ourselves kneeling in a row together at the altar rail. I realized we had never done this before as a family. Always in the past either Ali or I have been on the other side of the communion rail serving or have had to be elsewhere preaching or teaching. But here we were all together, with the exception of our second daughter, Kirsten, who was in Sri Lanka.

At lunch that day, I asked the family what they had been thinking at that moment in church when we knelt to receive. Was it not extraordinary to have been all together at the altar rail? Young Cameron was the first to respond. He said, "I was thinking of Kirsten." And the rest of us thought, what a thoughtful boy is this that he was thinking of his absent sister. But then Cameron said, "Well, I wasn't actually thinking about Kirsten. I wish I had been thinking about Kirsten."

Our Brendan was the next to respond. He spoke very simply and straightforwardly, as he does when he is freed from the anxieties of mental illness that so often haunt him. He said, "I felt whole." For one moment, for one fleeting moment, he felt whole. Edwin Muir, the Scottish poet, writes of such a moment. In his poem "The Transfiguration," when he glimpses within himself what he calls "the clear unfallen world," he says, "If it lasted but another moment it might have held for ever."[18]

Brendan felt whole. How do we enable one another to glimpse wholeness? And when such gifts of communion are given, how can we serve these moments of grace so that they last a bit longer, and in lasting a bit longer begin to take hold again so that deep change can occur from within us? Thomas Merton, at that same gathering in Bangkok over the last few days of his life, said to his religious peers from other traditions, "The deepest level of communication is not communication, but communion."[19] We do not have to discover a new unity. We do not have to construct a new foundation for peace. What we have to do is recover our original oneness, the essential unity that underlies our diversity. "We are already one," he said. "But we imagine that we are not." It is the glimpsing of this communion at the heart of life and the further releasing of it through love that will enable our transfiguration. The challenge is to become what we already essentially are—one.

CHAPTER 9

MAKING WHOLE
AGAIN

In 1941, Jane Owen climbed Indian Mound in southern Indiana. She had recently married Kenneth Owen of New Harmony, the little Midwestern town of nineteenth-century utopian fame. She was an oil heiress from Texas—wealthy, well educated, and cultured, but with no clear vision of how to use her riches. In fact, she felt at a loss as to what the focus of her life should be. So she brought questions with her to the top of the hill that day.

Indian Mound, on the edge of historic New Harmony, had been a sacred site of gathering for the Native American tribe of Shawnee. It is still a place to which individuals instinctively find their way to pray, as did Jane Owen that day. She felt like a stranger in a strange land. Even her name had recently changed. So at the top of the mound she prayed for clarity, and in the midst of her prayer began an imaginary inner conversation with someone else who had been a stranger in a strange land—Abraham. And he too had had a name change, from Abram to Abraham.

Within her imagination she was drawn to the story of Abraham building an altar in the foreign land of Moriah.

And she realized that this was what she was to do: build an altar of prayer for the world in New Harmony. It was this realization that led her eventually to commission the French sculptor Jacques Lipchitz to create his *Descent of the Spirit*. And as Lipchitz put it in his inscription on the back of the sculpture, this work was created "for the goodwill of all mankind that the spirit might prevail."

This was the beginning of the rebirth of New Harmony. The sculpture was not simply a piece of art. It was an altar for peace. The *Descent of the Spirit* was a financial sacrifice for Jane Owen, as was the building of the Roofless Church around it in years to come. And the purpose of the altar was to invite further sacrifice in the world, a giving of ourselves for peace. The vision of the whole project was the rediscovery of harmony between peoples, between traditions, between nations. And the cost of harmony in our lives and world is sacrifice. As the fourteenth-century teacher Meister Eckhart said, "How peacefully the universe would live if each part served the whole."[1]

Carl Jung says that "every true and deep love is a sacrifice."[2] It is a giving of ourselves freely to something more than our ego. In love we offer ourselves to a oneness that is greater than our separateness. The English word *sacrifice* comes from the Latin *sacrificare*, which means "to make holy." We make sacrifices in our lives in order to make whole again. It is the holiness of wholeness. It is the essential oneness of life. What is love calling us to be and to do at this point in our lives? What is the sacrifice required of us if we and our world are to be whole, if we are to find a new harmony?

It is significant that in much of the Protestant tradition of Western Christianity we have abandoned the use of the word *altar*, in large part because of its association with sacrifice. We speak instead of the communion table. We focus on the sharing of bread and wine as symbols of unity and as signs of Jesus. In part this was an historic reaction to medieval Catholicism's notion of the sacrifice of the mass, the idea of Christ's perpetual self-giving. But in both traditions we minimized the role of *our* sacrifice. Instead of seeing Jesus' self-giving as a revelation, a lifting of the veil to show us the costliness of serving at love's altar in our lives and world, we represented the cross primarily as freeing us from having to make sacrifice. And we ended up creating the impression that we can have communion without self-giving, and that therefore we can enjoy oneness with each other, oneness with the earth, oneness with God, without personal cost.

This was certainly the case for me as a young minister. I remember my first celebration of communion. I thought it was something that could happen within the four walls of the university chapel with little regard to whether or not there was self-giving happening in our lives individually and collectively. I had just started as chaplain at McMaster University in Canada. And I imagined that on the first Sunday evening of term we would have a full chapel of students and faculty celebrating communion together. I had been busy preparing for that first communion. I had put up posters all over the university campus. I had run off hundreds of service sheets. I had even persuaded my mother to make piles of cake for the many who would come back to the chaplain's residence after communion.

Nervously I paced back and forth in the vestry before the service. My beautiful new alb looked pristine in its whiteness. I had mapped out in my mind exactly what to say and do in the full chapel. Then at 7 P.M. as the bells chimed, I entered the sanctuary to an extravagant Bach organ prelude. And there seated in the front row of the chapel was half my congregation—Ali and my parents. A few rows behind them was the other half, two middle-aged men who were not connected to the university but who had learned there was going to be food afterwards. Then there was the organist up in the loft, and she was there because the university paid her to be there. I was in such a state of shock and disappointment that I desperately clung to my original game plan, which was to preach from the high pulpit using a full manuscript and to officiate at the sacrament from behind the raised communion table at the east end.

What had this to do with communion? I certainly did not experience oneness that evening. I am a believer in the value of small and intimate celebrations of communion. It is not just a matter of numbers and a full sanctuary. But something of transformative value will happen in a liturgy only when there is a connection with life, and only when there is a willingness to make the sacrifices that are necessary in our lives and world if there is to be oneness. That connection was missing for me early in my chaplaincy work. In time it came, but it came in relation to the development of community life and commitment. And it came especially with the arrival of Central American refugees and the decision by students and faculty members to help receive them into the country and to address politically the injustices behind the refugee crisis. We found ourselves caught up in a movement of love. It was a desire to make whole again.

It was especially on Iona in years to come that I powerfully experienced the connection between *sacrificare* and communion. Late in the 1980s, in the period leading up to the release of Nelson Mandela, we had visits on Iona from African National Congress students living in exile. Because of their involvement in the politically banned ANC liberation movement in South Africa, they were prevented from returning home. So Christmas and Easter were especially times when they would travel to the island to join us in community.

During one such week, news came through from South Africa that some of the ANC students' friends and colleagues had been killed in a political demonstration in Cape Town. The news was upsetting and shocking. We were aware in our life together that week of the pain of South Africa's brokenness. We used South African chants of lamentation and longing for freedom in our morning and evening prayers. And on the last evening, we gathered for communion around the long table in the abbey church. As I lifted the bread to break it, a sound of weeping broke out at the table. The ANC students in their grief were sobbing with pain. The breaking of the bread in the liturgy, when we remember Jesus' brokenness, was at the same time their brokenness and the world's brokenness.

I felt I could not proceed as usual with the service. The weeping was for those who had died. We needed time to mourn together. And the tears were a realization of the cost of love. We needed time to let this settle within us more deeply. So I paused, allowing us this sacred time to grieve and to consider. When we dispersed that evening, we did so in silence, many of us leaving with a sharpened awareness of the relationship between sacrifice and communion, between self-giving and the altar of love. "Every true and deep love," says Jung, "is a sacrifice."

The next morning as I stood at the jetty in the heavy rain waving off the ferry with its load of ANC students returning to the mainland, I overheard a conversation behind me. It was between two British visitors to the island. The one gentleman was saying to the other, "What a shame those Africans don't know how to control their emotions. They ruined the service at the abbey last night." My hood was up, protecting me from the rain, so they did not know who was standing in front of them. But maybe it would not have mattered. Perhaps I should have turned to challenge their words. But I did not. I was speechless.

When I returned to the house that morning on Iona, I found my young Brendan writing a letter to President de Klerk of South Africa. It said very simply, "Stop the hurting." At the age of six, Brendan had been present at communion the previous evening. He had heard the sobbing. He had made the connection. And intuitively he knew what to do. So he wrote a letter. It was a beautiful expression in a young boy of a heartfelt desire for change. How many such letters did President de Klerk receive? And who knows what part they played in transforming the life of a nation?

Jung says that the cross is a "Christian totality symbol."[3] It symbolizes the way of completeness in which the quadrants or four cardinal points of the whole are connected. It consists of a vertical line and a horizontal line intersecting. The vertical line joins what is above with what is below— heaven and earth, spirit and matter, the cosmos and the earth. The horizontal line joins what is on one side with what is on the other side—East and West, the masculine and the feminine, the interests of one nation and the life of another. At the center of the cross, the opposites meet. And in the Christian tradition the center of the cross is the place of self-giving. It is love that has the power to conjoin what is considered irreconcilable. It is sacrifice that brings together the so-called opposites. But this is not to be confused with the doctrine of propitiation in which Christ's death has often been imagined in Christianity to be a payment to God for the sins of the world. Rather the symbol is pointing to the nature of love itself. Oneness is costly. It will be born within us and among us only if we are willing to die to our separateness. As Jung says, we "must celebrate a Last Supper" with our ego.[4] Whether as nations or as individuals or as an entire species, we must choose to abandon ourselves to love.

In 1939 Jung had a dreamlike experience in the middle of the night. He woke and saw at the foot of his bed the figure of Christ on the cross "bathed in bright light."[5] And he saw that Christ's body was made of "greenish gold." It was for Jung a powerful vision and a disturbing one. The greenish gold of the dream, he realized, was the symbolic color for transformation in alchemical thought. It represented the *anima mundi* or the greening spirit that is within all things. Among medieval alchemists, it was this belief that led to the hope that base metals could be changed into gold, for all things shared the same golden essence of life. But for Jung it was a way of speaking of the human soul's capacity for transformation. Within every human being is life's sacred essence. And it is love, especially love's willingness to sacrifice, that holds the key to transformation, to release again life's essential oneness. The twelfth-century teacher Hildegard of Bingen expresses it similarly when she says that Jesus reveals "the greening power" of the soul.[6] He shows us the way of love, the truth of love, and the life of love. It is love that will release life's greening force again.

A number of years ago on personal retreat, I used a form of contemplation developed by Ignatius of Loyola in the sixteenth century. Ignatius had discovered that the imagination was a faculty of knowing. He realized also that it could be a tool of fantasy, a way of escaping reality. But the significance of his discovery was the realization that our imagination could take us to places within ourselves to which the rational mind alone does not have access. Ignatius developed a form of contemplation in which he was able to make an imaginal connection between Jesus and himself. Specifically it was a way of contemplation in which he imaginatively placed himself in the Gospel stories of Jesus. He would allow the senses of his imagination to color the place, to people the narrative, and to bring him into direct conversation with Jesus.

This was the form of contemplation I used on retreat at St. Beuno's spirituality center in the north of Wales, the monastery where the poet Gerard Manley Hopkins studied for the priesthood and wrote some of his greatest poetry. In the time of contemplation, I used a story from St. Mark's Gospel in which Jesus is described as rising early in the morning "while it was still very dark" in order to go to a deserted place to pray (Mark 1:35). In my imagination I allowed the place to be a little bay off the Sound of Iona with which I am familiar. The time was early morning, just as the seagulls were beginning to announce the coming light. And I was a disciple wanting to be with Jesus in the silence of dawn.

I could not make him out on the shore. It was still too dark. There was only enough light to glimpse the barest outline of his form. I did not want to disturb him. My desire was simply to share in the silence. But in my imagination Jesus spoke to me. And his voice did not sound kindly. "What is it you want?" he asked. "I want to be with you," I replied. To which Jesus responded, "You don't know what you are asking." The light of dawn was growing. I was able to see a bit more of his shape. I now saw that he was doubled over like an old man, leaning on a stick. And then he began to be dismembered, losing one limb after another, until finally all that was left of him was a clump of seaweed against a wet rock on the shore.

It was a disturbing contemplation for me. At first I tried to dismiss its details from my mind. I even tried to reshape the story, retracing its stages and attempting to force my imagination in other directions. But in the end I could see nothing but the clump of seaweed on the strand. And I began to realize that truly I had not known what I was asking for. Part of me had wanted to be with Jesus on the shore. I liked the idea of getting away from the crowds as Jesus had done in the Gospel story. But what I had not realized was that to join Jesus in prayer was to approach the place of dismemberment. Prayer or meditative practice is about being dis-membered in order to be re-membered. It is about descending into the death of the ego in order to be reborn from our true depths. It is about being stripped down to our essence, where we will find the gold of our being, the greening power of the soul.

Jung says that to find our true self "involves a passion of the ego."[7] It is about letting go of the pretense of separateness, whether as individuals or as nations or communities. It is about "ex-centration," as Teilhard de Chardin calls it, a finding of our true center not simply within the limited confines of our own individuality but at the heart of one another as well.[8] It is not about ceasing to love ourselves but about loving ourselves in a radically new way, by loving the other as our self. It is, says Teilhard, about shifting "the axis" of our being outside of ourselves.[9] And in all of this it is about knowing that our essence is like the precious seaweed gathered on the shores of the Western Isles of Scotland each year to fertilize the fields for the next year's growth and fecundity. This is the wisdom of Jesus that I heard again in my imagination on the shores of Iona. "Unless a grain of wheat falls into the earth and dies, it remains a single grain; but if it dies, it bears much fruit" (John 12:24). It is only as our separating ego is dis-membered that we will re-member our true self, one with all selves.

A few years ago, we had a visit in Edinburgh from Jon Sobrino, the Jesuit priest and liberation theologian from El Salvador. Jon had been a member of the Jesuit community at the University of Central America in San Salvador that experienced martyrdom in November 1989. Jon happened to be out of the country at the time, but six of his Jesuit brothers as well as the housekeeper and her daughter were assassinated. Members of the Salvadoran military broke into the Jesuit rectory and brutally murdered them because of their outspoken opposition to the human rights abuses of the ruling government junta.

During the public address that Jon Sobrino delivered in Edinburgh, he was asked by a member of the audience what he thought of the phrase from Christian Scripture that the death of Jesus was "according to the will of our God and Father" (Galatians 1:4). Sobrino answered, "Of course it was the will of the Father that the Son should die. It was the will of the Father that the Son should love." Jesus died because he loved his people and his nation enough to speak against the injustices that were being perpetrated by the holders of political and religious power. It was the will of God that Jesus should love. And it was because he loved that he died, not to atone an angry God but to serve at the altar of love for his people.

Jon Sobrino was a friend of Archbishop Oscar Romero, who was assassinated by a government death squad in March 1980 as he celebrated communion in the chapel of La Divina Providencia hospital in San Salvador. He was shot while lifting the chalice during the Eucharist, having just uttered the words of the mass, "This is my lifeblood poured out for you." Romero's blood and the wine of the spilled chalice mingled on the white cloth of the altar of sacrifice.

Jon Sobrino was asked why Oscar Romero died. "He died," said Sobrino, "because every week in the Cathedral of San Salvador he would publicly name those who had been murdered at the hands of government death squads. And he died," continued Sobrino, "not only because he named those who had been murdered. He died because he named those who were responsible." It was the will of God that Romero should love his people, and he died doing so.

Teilhard de Chardin taught that just as Jesus bore the sins of his nation, so are we to bear the cost of this moment in time. "Serving the world," he said, "is hard to bear, like a cross." But "a price has to be paid for the struggle."[10] Who will take responsibility for the plight of the earth and its species, for the journey of our nations and religions, for the well-being of our families and communities? We have the ability to respond. We have response-ability. Will we take it up? It is the will of God that we should love. It is the will of God that we should make whole again. For Teilhard it was a matter of holding together "the yearnings of the soul and the demands of the universe."[11] It is a matter of allowing our deepest desires to become one with the deepest needs of the world. Only thus will we be truly satisfied. Our individual aspirations, says Teilhard, can only be "fulfilled in the realization of the whole."[12] It is in sacrificing our separateness that we will discover our wholeness.

On Iona, one of the high-standing crosses in front of the abbey is St. Martin's Cross, with its distinctive Celtic feature of cross form and circle form combined as a way of pointing to the oneness of Christ and creation. At the heart of St. Martin's Cross, where the vertical line and the horizontal line intersect, is an image of the Mother and Child. She holds the child against her breast. She has paid the price of labor and now holds the newborn close to her. She has born the pain of giving birth. And now she will sustain the child with her own being, with the milk of her love. In the Celtic world it is said that there is a mother's heart at the heart of God. At the heart of a mother's heart is the willingness to make sacrifice for her child. It is a revelation of the very heart of God's being. And it is a revelation also of the human heart made in the image of God's heart.

In *Christ of the Celts* I tell the story of being brushed by an eagle. I had been hiking up an arroyo in New Mexico, and as I bent to pass under a fallen pine tree, I was met by an eagle swooping toward me with a rabbit in her talons. Either she had not noticed me or was so intent on the catch that she was not bothered by my presence. So we met under the tree's fallen trunk, and her strong wing touched my left arm. It was an exhilarating experience, to have physical contact with this untamed icon of heaven. I was aware also that it was a spiritual experience, for in Christian symbolism the eagle is associated with John the Beloved, who sees with a height of unitary vision the oneness of all things. But the most important part of the story I did not tell in *Christ of the Celts*, for it had not yet happened.

After my eagle experience, there was someone in particular with whom I wanted to share the story. It was Ronald Royball, a native musician and storyteller from Santa Fe. We had met years earlier, and he had told me about a life-changing dream in which a great eagle had swept down from the sky to touch his hand with its wing tip. When Ronald woke, he realized he was to be a musician, playing the native flute and sharing the wisdom of his people through music and story.

So it was Ronald whom I especially wanted to tell. He joined me for lunch close to the arroyo where I had hiked the previous year. And with some pride I told him in great detail about everything that had happened, and showed him exactly where on my arm the eagle had brushed against me. When finally I finished, Ronald said, "John Philip, I want you to think about the rabbit. The rabbit is Christ. The rabbit connected you and the eagle. The rabbit made heaven and earth one for you. And he lost his life doing so. I want you to think about the rabbit. The rabbit is Christ." He spoke not one word to me about the eagle!

When I heard Ronald's words, I knew he was right. I had missed the main point of the story. Yes, of course, I shall always be thrilled to know that I was brushed by an eagle. But I would not have met the eagle without the sacrifice of the rabbit. This is not to say that every part of the story can be directly applied spiritually. The rabbit did not choose to offer itself, although Native American wisdom would probably perceive an element of choice in all of nature's sacrifices. But Ronald's words prompted me to ask more deeply what this experience was about. His words prompted me to ask what the costly connections are that I am to make in my life. What are the costly connections we are to make? The encounter with the eagle was a meeting also with the rabbit.

In 2007 there was a terrorist attack at Glasgow International Airport in Scotland. Ali and our younger son, Cameron, were traveling that day. They arrived at the airport just minutes before the Jeep that had been packed with explosives drove through the front window of the terminal and burst into flames. If they had arrived a few minutes later, they would have been checking in at exactly that spot in the airport. As it was, they were inside the terminal getting close to the ticket counter. Then suddenly in front of them hundreds of people were running in the opposite direction. Ahead of them they glimpsed the Jeep and one of the terrorists on fire.

People were desperately running to get away. Our son-in-law Mark was with Ali and Cameron. He had taken them to the airport and was helping with their luggage. He said, "Drop your bags. Run." As the three of them ran, Mark, in later recounting what was going on in his mind, said, "I was listening for the moment of explosion. I was trying to decide when to throw myself over Cameron."

This was not Mark boasting. This was a candid, straightforward expression of his heart. He would not put it this way because he does not claim to be religious. But for me this was an expression of the heart of God. It was an expression of the true depths of the human soul. Deep within us is the desire to love.

In the end, the explosives did not detonate. Scotland was spared the sort of carnage that many places in our world are subjected to on a regular basis. How can we be part of transformation in our world so that such acts of terror do not pull us further apart? For us as a family, we will always remember Mark's willingness to risk himself for Cameron. It was the antithesis of the fear and hatred that motivated the bomb plot. How can we nurture the willingness to sacrifice? In other words, how can we nourish the desire to love, a desire that is within us all, although often confined to the smallest circles of relationship and family, yet a desire that can be equally although more challengingly applied to broader spheres of relationship in our world? There are many stages to transformation, including the detailed decisions of how to reenvision and restructure the relationships of life, whether between nations and species or between individuals and communities. But unless there is a willingness to be compassionate and to bear the cost of love, we will move nowhere except into further separation and division.

Recently I had a dream in which there were many people gathered together in a large open space. They were each given a circle of fabric, and it was understood that they were to form a single large circle or mandala out of their separate pieces, but there were to be no gaps between the pieces. It was like a giant jigsaw in which every piece was to fit perfectly together. At first there was great frustration. As circle was placed against circle, many holes appeared in the pattern. Then there came a moment of realization. People became aware that there was "a first circle," as they called it, and that all of their separate circles needed to be placed around the first circle to produce the complete pattern. In the dream it was not clear where the first circle had come from. But it was agreed that it should be the center and that the other circles should relate to the form of the first circle. The separate pieces therefore needed to be refashioned in order to fit together. There were to be no straight lines in the pieces because there were no straight lines in the first circle. What then began to emerge was a single interconnected pattern. Each separate circle was reshaped, folded into curves, so that it could be positioned into the curves of other refashioned circles. In the dream I did not see the finished mandala, but I knew it was coming and that it would be complete.

For me this was a dream about sacrifice. It was about being refashioned into a single pattern of wholeness. It spoke of the costs and creativity of being re-formed in relation to one another. But the dream also stirred in me an awareness of the original pattern deep in life, "the first circle" as the dream had put it. No one in the dream knew exactly where this original pattern had come from. None of us, whether as individuals or traditions or nations, possess it. It was simply in our midst. Our separate pieces were like the first circle, but it was only together that we could form the complete pattern. We needed one another's willingness to sacrifice.

Last year I gave some talks at a church in Minneapolis. Before the opening session, I was seated in a side chapel close to the main auditorium preparing myself in silence. The talks were going to touch on themes of sacrifice, of making whole again. And I was going to raise specific questions in relation to wholeness. Do we want to be part of transformation? And what are the costs of change, both individually and collectively? As I sat pondering these themes, I noticed on the front wall of the chapel a traditional Ethiopian cross with its large diamond shape at the top and narrow shaft connecting to a smaller square shape at the bottom. And I realized it was like a big key hanging on the wall in front of me.

In the Christian tradition, our key is the cross, or what Jung calls "the Christian totality symbol." It opens for us the way of love, the truth of love, and the life of love. It connects for us what has been considered opposite—heaven and earth, the divine and the human, the one and the many, God and all things. It is the key of love. It is the key to transformation.

This may begin to make it all sound simple. And I suppose it is simple. But it is not easy. The difficulty comes in using the key. The challenge ensues in taking it off the wall of our religious symbolism and making use of it in the relationships of our lives and the wider world. The test is in whether we choose to use it again and again and again, resisting the delusion that we will be well by looking after ourselves in isolation, by tending our own nation, our own species, our own tradition, to the neglect of the whole. It is what Teilhard de Chardin calls "the primacy of humility," the greatness of bowing in love to what is deepest in one another.[13]

The way of sacrifice cannot be imposed, for it is the way of love. By its very nature it must be chosen. Hildegard says that we are "to act through the kiss of choice."[14] This is what ANC students did in loving their nation and paying the price of exile. This is what Jon Sobrino and his fellow Jesuits did in speaking out against the political abuses of El Salvador. They kissed the key to love. This is what our Mark did in the Glasgow terrorist attack in his willingness to sacrifice. What is it that we will choose, and how can we strengthen one another to make this "kiss of choice"?

In one of my last conversations with Jane Owen before she died in the summer of 2010, she said, "New Harmony saved me." Some would be excused for thinking that I had misheard her. Was it not Jane Owen who had saved New Harmony? Was it not her conviction that had turned around this forgotten little town, transforming it into a place of new vision for the world? History will record what many people have already said, that Jane Owen saved New Harmony. And they are right. That is part of the truth. But a deeper part of the story is that New Harmony saved her. "New Harmony saved me," she said, "because it taught me how to love." She was a rich young woman from Texas, but here she found the objects of her love—the people, the place, the vision of a new harmony. It was here that she learned how to sacrifice. And so it was here that she truly found herself.

This is the deeper part of the story in all great lives. Many will say that Nelson Mandela saved South Africa. But Nelson Mandela would be the first to say that South Africa saved him. In the people of South Africa he found the object of his love, and in giving himself for them he found his true stature of soul. Many would say that Oscar Romero saved El Salvador. And this is part of the story. But the deeper truth is that his love for the people of El Salvador saved Oscar Romero. And in the Christian household, we hear again and again in word and song that Jesus saved the world. But must we not also say that the hidden part of the story is that the world saved Jesus? Because Jesus found in the world the true object of his love, and in giving himself in love, he found himself forever.

What is it that will save us? Who are the people, the creatures, the lands, the nations that will awaken our compassion, and who in awakening our love will awaken our willingness to make whole again? These are the ones who hold the hidden part of the story in our search for wholeness. These are the ones in whom we will find the key to love.

EPILOGUE

Casa del Sol is a little spirituality center in the high desert of New Mexico. It is committed, as our vision statement says, to "seeking the oneness of the human soul and the healing of creation." At its service of blessing in 2006, we gathered in the courtyard of the old hacienda and sounded a large set of wind chimes in the four directions—south, west, north, and east. From the whole earth we were seeking the Spirit of new beginnings. As the chimes rang out in each of the four cardinal directions, Jim Baird, our director of program, recited words from the prophecy of Isaiah: "I am about to do a new thing. Now it springs forth. Do you not perceive it?" (Isaiah 43:19). By the time we got to the east, the direction of light and fresh beginnings, Jim's voice carried powerfully over the desert landscape, "I am about to do a new thing. Now it springs forth. Do you not perceive it?"

Paul Tillich, the great German theologian who as early as the 1950s was prophetically announcing God as Ground of being, preached on these words from Isaiah. In his sermon, he said that as long as we think the new thing can

only come through the old thing, then we will likely miss
the new thing. He was not saying that the new thing cannot
come through the old thing. He was not saying, for instance,
that the new consciousness of earth's oneness cannot be
born from within the inherited language and thought forms
of our religion and culture. He was saying, however, that if
we assume that the Holy Wind of new beginnings can only
come through our existing religious and cultural traditions,
then we will likely miss the new thing. "It is not the old
which creates the new," he said. "All we can do is to be
ready for it."[1] How do we get ready to open to the new
Pentecost, to the new thing that the Spirit is doing in the
earth and the human soul?

On the afternoon of the dedication of Casa del Sol, I
was out jogging across the high desert. My mind was elsewhere, remembering the wind chimes of the morning and
thinking ahead to how Casa del Sol might serve the "new
thing" that the Spirit is doing. I was enjoying the rhythm
of my heart and breath and body pumping together as one.
Visually I was aware of something on the path in front of
me, but my mind gave it no attention. It seemed nothing
more than a dead branch. When I was halfway over it,
however, it coiled and rattled. My heart accelerated, as did
my legs. I was so frightened that I did not even look back.

Presumably the diamondback rattlesnake could easily
have struck me. It must have just wanted to warn me. I
felt sufficiently warned and ever since have kept my eyes
closely peeled to the landscape when moving across the
high desert. But it did not take me long that day to realize
that this visitation had another significance for me as well.

The synchronicity of meeting with a rattlesnake on the same day as praying for new beginnings in our world was too great to ignore.

In many cultures, including the world of Native American thought, the snake is a symbol of healing. It is wise concerning the plants and herbs of the earth, and its venom can be used medicinally. We wanted Casa del Sol to be part of healing in the world, and we wanted its vision and work to be grounded in a close relationship to the earth. The rattlesnake is known for its strong protective instinct and its rattle of warning. We wanted Casa del Sol to be part of a prophetic warning in our world of the need to change direction if we are to avoid catastrophe. And the snake is known for its practice of shedding its skin in order to grow and to shed parasites and infections that have attached to the old skin. We wanted the community of Casa del Sol to be part of learning how to shed old forms that prevent new growth and transformation in our world. And the rattlesnake's distinctive rattles are in fact formed by the shedding of its skin. We will find a prophetic role in life only if we are prepared to shed aspects of what we have become, whether as individuals or as traditions or as a species.

The myths at the heart of our culture and religion will die if they do not continue to grow and change form. The beliefs and stories that are cherished in our communities and churches as giving central expression to life's meaning and mystery need to be clothed anew in every age. As Jung says, we need to "dream the myth onwards."[2] And at this point in time we will meaningfully dream the myth onwards only if we include in the most important vocabulary and symbolism of our rituals and articulation of faith the growing awareness of life's essential oneness. We will live and be well as a species and as an earth community only to the extent that we shed the beliefs and the practices that are tearing us apart rather than re-forming us together.

Throughout this book I have spoken of us living at "a moment of grace," as Thomas Berry calls it. We are living in the midst of an awareness of earth's oneness, the likes of which humanity has never known. We have been given a way of seeing that has enormous consequences for the transformation and healing of our lives and world. But as Berry says, "moments of grace are transient moments."[3] We will either choose to meet this moment and translate its grace into the relationships of our lives and nations, or we will lose this moment and abandon ourselves further and further to fragmentations and lack of well-being. Which will it be?

The Scottish poet Edwin Muir in his poem "All We" uses the image of marriage to point to our relationship with the earth. "We gave and took the ring," he says, "and pledged ourselves to the earth."[4] This is the pledge we are to make today if we are to be well. This is the pledge we are to make as individuals and communities, as nations and as a species. Our wellness belongs inseparably together. It relates directly to the oneness of the earth and the interrelatedness of everything that has being. "All we like sheep have gone astray," says the prophecy of Isaiah. "We have all turned to our own way" (Isaiah 53:6). We have thought we could find wholeness separately. We have thought we could be well in isolation. But in this moment of grace, "all we" are being invited to take the ring of oneness and to pledge ourselves to the earth and to one another in radically new ways.

A new harmony: the Spirit, the earth, and the human soul. The Spirit is doing a new thing. It is springing forth now in our consciousness, among every people, in every discipline, in every walk of life. Do we see it? And shall we serve it? A new Pentecost is stirring in the human soul. Will we open to this moment of grace and be led into relationships of oneness we could never before have imagined?

NOTES

Prologue

1. C. G. Jung, *Mysterium Coniunctionis* (Princeton, NJ: Princeton University Press, 1989), p. 180.

2. R. Johnson, *Balancing Heaven and Earth* (San Francisco: HarperSanFrancisco, 1998), p. 10.

3. J. S. Eriugena, *Periphyseon* [The division of nature], trans. J. O'Meara (Montreal: Bellarmin, 1987), p. 293.

4. Ibid., p. 29.

5. D. Bohm, *Wholeness and the Implicate Order* (London: Routledge, 1980), p. xi.

6. C. G. Jung, *Memories, Dreams, Reflections* (New York: Vintage, 1989), p. 39.

7. Johnson, *Balancing Heaven and Earth*, p. 291.

8. Meister Eckhart, *Selected Treatises and Sermons*, trans. J. M. Clark and J. V. Skinner (London: Fount, 1994), p. 84.

9. C. G. Jung, *Psychology and Religion* (Princeton, NJ: Princeton University Press, 1975), p. 180.

10. Ibid., p. 186.

11. Julian of Norwich, *Revelations of Divine Love*, trans. E. Spearing (London: Penguin, 1998), p. 129.

12. Ibid., p. 83.

13. B. R. Rees, ed., *The Letters of Pelagius and His Followers* (Woodbridge, England: Boydell Press, 1991), p. 45.

14. B. Layton, ed., *The Gnostic Scriptures* (London: SCM, 1987), p. 50.

15. Eriugena, *Periphyseon*, p. 692.

16. Jung, *Psychology and Religion*, p. 89.

17. T. Berry, *The Great Work* (New York: Bell Tower, 1999), p. 198.

Chapter One: Every Bush Is Burning

1. C. G. Jung, *Civilization in Transition* (New York: Bollingen, 1964), p. 528.

2. Meister Eckhart, *Teacher and Preacher*, trans. B. McGinn (Mahwah, NJ: Paulist Press, 1986), p. 172.

3. Meister Eckhart, *Selected Treatises and Sermons*, trans. J. M. Clark and J. V. Skinner (London: Fount, 1994), p. 167.

4. Ibid., p. 44.

5. Ibid., p. 62.

6. M. Fox, ed., *Hildegard of Bingen's Book of Divine Works* (Santa Fe, NM: Bear & Company, 1987), p. 132.

7. Ibid., p. 273.

8. Ibid., p. 359.

9. J. S. Eriugena, *Periphyseon* [The division of nature], trans. J. O'Meara (Montreal: Bellarmin, 1987), p. 38.

10. K. White, "The House of Insight," in *The Bird Path: Collected Longer Poems* (Edinburgh: Mainstream, 1989), p. 145.

11. D. Bohm, *Wholeness and the Implicate Order* (London: Routledge, 1980), p. 11.

12. R. Grant, ed., *Irenaeus of Lyons* (London: Routledge, 1997), p. 150.

13. Ibid., p. 151.

14. Ibid., p. 169.

15. R. Ferguson, ed., *Daily Readings with George MacLeod* (London: Fount, 1991), p. 74.

16. G. M. Hopkins, "God's Grandeur," in *Poems and Prose of Gerard Manley Hopkins*, ed. W. H. Gardner (London: Penguin, 1970), p. 27.

17. Fox, *Hildegard of Bingen's Book of Divine Works*, pp. 80, 101.

18. Hopkins, *Poems and Prose*.

19. Ibid., p. 27.

20. Fox, *Hildegard of Bingen's Book of Divine Works*, p. 8.

21. Jung, *Civilization in Transition*, p. 518.

Chapter Two: Outbursts of Singularity

1. E. Muir, "Day and Night," in *Collected Poems* (London: Faber, 1984), p. 240.

2. P. Teilhard de Chardin, *The Heart of Matter*, trans. R. Hague (London: Collins, 1978), p. 50.

3. C. G. Jung, *The Archetypes and the Collective Unconscious* (London: Routledge, 1990), p. 178.

4. R. Johnson, *Balancing Heaven and Earth* (San Francisco: HarperSanFrancisco, 1998), p. 81.

5. Jung, *Archetypes and the Collective Unconscious*, p. 253.

6. C. G. Jung, *Memories, Dreams, Reflections* (New York: Vintage, 1989), p. 394.

7. C. G. Jung, *Mysterium Coniunctionis* (Princeton, NJ: Princeton University Press, 1989), p. 367.

8. Ibid., pp. 370–371.

9. A. Heschel, *Who Is Man?* (Palo Alto, CA: Stanford University Press, 1965), p. 38.

10. Meister Eckhart, *Teacher and Preacher*, trans. B. McGinn (Mahwah, NJ: Paulist Press, 1986), p. 189.

11. M. Fox, ed., *Hildegard of Bingen's Book of Divine Works* (Santa Fe, NM: Bear & Company, 1987), p. 343.

Chapter Three: Keep on Remembering

1. C. G. Jung, *Aspects of the Feminine* (London: Ark, 1992), p. 44.

2. M. Fox, ed., *Hildegard of Bingen's Book of Divine Works* (Santa Fe, NM: Bear & Company, 1987), p. 145.

3. Ibid., p. 90.

4. P. Teilhard de Chardin, *Le Milieu Divin*, trans. R. Hague (London: Collins, 1967), p. 111.

5. Ibid., p. 115.

6. Ibid., p. 131.

7. P. Teilhard de Chardin, "Cosmic Life," in *The Prayer of the Universe*, trans. R. Hague (London: Collins, 1977), p. 103.

8. Meister Eckhart, *Teacher and Preacher*, trans. B. McGinn (Mahwah, NJ: Paulist Press, 1986), p. 54.

9. G. Macdonald, *Lilith* (Grand Rapids, MI: Eerdmans, 1981), p. 81.

10. K. White, "The House of Insight," in *The Bird Path: Collected Longer Poems* (Edinburgh: Mainstream, 1989), p. 141.

11. Ibid., p. 146.

12. A. Heschel, *Who Is Man?* (Palo Alto, CA: Stanford University Press, 1965), p. 78.

13. P. Epstein, *Kabbalah: The Way of the Jewish Mystic* (Boston: Shambhala, 1988), p. 157.

14. M. Weber, "Science as a Vocation," in *From Max Weber: Essays on Sociology*, trans. H. Gerth and C. Wright Mills (New York: Oxford University Press, 1946), p. 139.

15. G. F. MacLeod, *The Whole Earth Shall Cry Glory* (Glasgow: Wild Goose Publications, 1985), p. 60.

16. T. Dorgan, "The Promised Garden," in *The Ordinary House of Love* (Galway: Salmon, 1992), p. 75.

17. W. Blake, "Jerusalem," in *The Complete Poetry and Prose of William Blake*, ed. D. Eerdman (New York: Doubleday, 1988), p. 158.

18. T. Berry, *The Great Work* (New York: Bell Tower, 1999), p. 175.

Chapter Four: Looking Suffering Straight in the Face

1. E. Hillesum, *An Interrupted Life: The Diaries and Letters of Etty Hillesum 1941–1943*, trans. A. J. Pomerans (London: Persephone, 1999), p. 164.

2. Ibid., p. 164.

3. Ibid., p. 37.

4. M. Fox, ed., *Hildegard of Bingen's Book of Divine Works* (Santa Fe, NM: Bear & Company, 1987), p. 350.

5. T. Berry, *The Great Work* (New York: Bell Tower, 1999), p. 164.

6. Julian of Norwich, *Revelations of Divine Love*, trans. E. Spearing (London: Penguin, 1998), p. 169.

7. Ibid., p. 119.

8. C. G. Jung, *Aspects of the Feminine* (London: Ark, 1992), p. 72.

9. E. Muir, "The Cloud," in *Collected Poems* (London: Faber, 1984), p. 246.

10. Hillesum, *An Interrupted Life*, p. 186.

11. Ibid., p. 189.

Chapter Five: Digging God Out

1. E. Hillesum, *An Interrupted Life: The Diaries and Letters of Etty Hillesum 1941–1943*, trans. A. J. Pomerans (London: Persephone, 1999), p. 242.

2. Ibid., p. 249.

3. Ibid., p. 250.

4. Ibid., p. 53.

5. P. Tillich, *The Courage to Be* (London: Collins, 1952), p. 154.

6. M. Fox, ed., *Hildegard of Bingen's Book of Divine Works* (Santa Fe, NM: Bear & Company, 1987), p. 209.

7. Ibid., p. 209.

8. J. S. Eriugena, *Periphyseon* [The division of nature], trans. J. O'Meara (Montreal: Bellarmin, 1987), p. 643.

9. C. G. Jung, *Mysterium Coniunctionis* (Princeton, NJ: Princeton University Press, 1989), p. 387.

10. P. Teilhard de Chardin, *Christianity and Evolution*, trans. R. Hague (London: Collins, 1971), p. 150.

11. Meister Eckhart, *Teacher and Preacher*, trans. B. McGinn (Mahwah, NJ: Paulist Press, 1986), p. 268.

12. Meister Eckhart, *Selected Treatises and Sermons*, trans. J. M. Clark and J. V. Skinner (London: Fount, 1994), p. 189.

13. Ibid., p. 189.

14. Hillesum, *An Interrupted Life*, p. 218.

15. Ibid., p. 218.

16. Ibid., p. 218.

Chapter Six: A Balm for All Wounds

1. E. Hillesum, *An Interrupted Life: The Diaries and Letters of Etty Hillesum 1941–1943*, trans. A. J. Pomerans (London: Persephone, 1999), p. 301.

2. Ibid., p. 312.

3. Ibid., p. 402.

4. Ibid., p. 267.

5. Ibid., p. 282.

6. C. G. Jung, *Psychology and Religion* (Princeton, NJ: Princeton University Press, 1975), p. 179.

7. C. G. Jung, *Memories, Dreams, Reflections* (New York: Vintage, 1989), p. 175.

8. Ibid., p. 176.

9. T. Berry, *The GreatWork* (NewYork: BellTower, 1999), p. 199.

10. Jung, *Psychology and Religion*, p. 155.

11. C. G. Jung, *Mysterium Coniunctionis* (Princeton, NJ: Princeton University Press, 1989), p. 428.

12. K. White, "The House at the Head of the Tides," in *The Bird Path* (Edinburgh: Mainstream, 1989), p. 236.

13. E. Muir, "One Foot in Eden," in *Collected Poems* (London: Faber, 1984), p. 227.

14. Ibid., p. 227.

15. Julian of Norwich, *Revelations of Divine Love*, trans. E. Spearing (London: Penguin, 1998), p. 80.

16. Ibid., p. 3.

17. Ibid., p. 86.

18. Ibid., p. 89.

19. A. W. Haddan and W. Stubbs, eds., *Councils and Ecclesiastical Documents Relating to Great Britain and Ireland*, vol. 2 (Oxford: Oxford University Press, 1873), p. 120.

20. M. Fox, ed., *Hildegard of Bingen's Book of DivineWorks* (Santa Fe, NM: Bear & Company, 1987), p. 101.

21. Jung, *Mysterium Coniunctionis*, p. 193.

22. Jung, *Memories, Dreams, Reflections*, p. 134.

23. Amnesty International, *Honduras: José Eduardo Lopez: 20 Years Later: It Is Time for Justice*, March 30, 2001, www.amnesty.org/en/

library/asset/AMR37/002/2001/en/5f5188d8-d951-11dd-a057-592cb671dd8b/amr370022001en.pdf.

24. Ibid.

25. Hillesum, *An Interrupted Life*, p. 355.

26. Ibid., p. 227.

27. Ibid., p. 395.

28. Ibid., p. 426.

29. Ibid., p. 355.

Chapter Seven: A Pearl of Great Price

1. P. Teilhard de Chardin, *Le Milieu Divin*, trans. R. Hague (London: Collins, 1967), p. 116.

2. C. G. Jung, *Mysterium Coniunctionis* (Princeton, NJ: Princeton University Press, 1989), p. 369.

3. P. Teilhard de Chardin, *Christianity and Evolution*, trans. R. Hague (London: Collins, 1971), p. 171.

4. P. Teilhard de Chardin, *The Heart of Matter*, trans. R. Hague (London: Collins, 1978), p. 50.

5. U. King, *Spirit of Fire: The Life and Vision of Teilhard de Chardin* (New York: Orbis, 1996), p. 145.

6. T. Berry, *The Great Work* (New York: Bell Tower, 1999), p. 17.

7. R. Tarnas, *Cosmos and Psyche: Intimations of a New World View* (New York: Plume, 2007), p. 484.

8. Meister Eckhart, *Selected Treatises and Sermons*, trans. J. M. Clark and J. V. Skinner (London: Fount, 1994), p. 180.

9. Jung, *Mysterium Coniunctionis*, p. 200.

10. P. Teilhard de Chardin, "The Eternal Feminine," in *The Prayer of the Universe*, trans. R. Hague (London: Collins, 1977), p. 143.

11. Tarnas, *Cosmos and Psyche*, p. 25.

12. R. A. Culpepper, *John, the Son of Zebedee: The Life of a Legend* (Minneapolis, MN: Fortress Press, 2000), p. 165.

13. Ibid., p. 165.

14. Jung, *Mysterium Coniunctionis*, p. 536.

15. A. Carmichael, *Carmina Gadelica* (Edinburgh: Floris Classics, 1994), p. 73.

16. P. Teilhard de Chardin, "Cosmic Life," in *The Prayer of the Universe*, trans. R. Hague (London: Collins, 1977), p. 103.

Chapter Eight: Rediscovering an Older Unity

1. N. Burton, P. Hart, and J. Laughlin, eds., *The Asian Journal of Thomas Merton* (New York: New Directions, 1975), p. 308.

2. Ibid., p. 308.

3. Meister Eckhart, *Teacher and Preacher*, trans. B. McGinn (Mahwah, NJ: Paulist Press, 1986), p. 226.

4. Meister Eckhart, *Selected Treatises and Sermons*, trans. J. M. Clark and J. V. Skinner (London: Fount, 1994), p. 132.

5. T. Berry, *The Great Work* (New York: Bell Tower, 1999), p. 147.

6. Eckhart, *Selected Treatises and Sermons*, p. 182.

7. P. Teilhard de Chardin, "Cosmic Life," in *The Prayer of the Universe*, trans. R. Hague (London: Collins, 1977), p. 51.

8. Julian of Norwich, *Showings of Divine Love*, trans. E. Colledge and J. Walsh (Mahwah: Paulist Press, 1978), pp. 290, 302.

9. M. Fox, ed., *Hildegard of Bingen's Book of Divine Works* (Santa Fe, NM: Bear & Company, 1987), p. 204.

10. Ibid., p. 11.

11. Ibid., p. 87.

12. C. G. Jung, *Mysterium Coniunctionis* (Princeton, NJ: Princeton University Press, 1989), p. 459.

13. Ibid., p. 478.

14. Eckhart, *Selected Treatises and Sermons*, p. 115.

15. Teilhard, "Cosmic Life," p. 82.

16. Berry, *The Great Work*, p. 198.

17. Fox, *Hildegard of Bingen's Book of Divine Works*, p. 80.

18. E. Muir, "The Transfiguration," in *Collected Poems* (London: Faber, 1984), pp. 198–199.

19. Burton, Hart, and Laughlin, *The Asian Journal of Thomas Merton*, p. 308.

Chapter Nine: Making Whole Again

1. Meister Eckhart, *Teacher and Preacher*, trans. B. McGinn (Mahwah, NJ: Paulist Press, 1986), p. 218.

2. C. G. Jung, *Aspects of the Feminine* (London: Ark, 1992), p. 39.

3. C. G. Jung, *Mysterium Coniunctionis* (Princeton, NJ: Princeton University Press, 1989), p. 101.

4. Ibid., p. 364.

5. C. G. Jung, *Memories, Dreams, Reflections* (New York: Vintage, 1989), p. 210.

6. M. Fox, ed., *Hildegard of Bingen's Book of Divine Works* (Santa Fe, NM: Bear & Company, 1987), p. 244.

7. C. G. Jung, *Psychology and Religion* (Princeton, NJ: Princeton University Press, 1975), p. 157.

8. P. Teilhard de Chardin, *Le Milieu Divin*, trans. R. Hague (London: Collins, 1967), p. 88.

9. P. Teilhard de Chardin, "Cosmic Life," in *The Prayer of the Universe*, trans. R. Hague (London: Collins, 1977), p. 72.

10. Ibid., pp. 99, 100.

11. Ibid., p. 76.

12. Ibid., p. 76.

13. Ibid., p. 86.

14. Fox, *Hildegard of Bingen's Book of Divine Works*, p. 227.

Epilogue

1. P. Tillich, *The Shaking of the Foundations* (London: Penguin, 1966), pp. 182–183.

2. C. G. Jung, *The Archetypes and the Collective Unconscious* (London: Routledge, 1990), p. 160.

3. T. Berry, *The Great Work* (New York: Bell Tower, 1999), p. 201.

4. E. Muir, "All We," in *Collected Poems* (London: Faber, 1984), p. 158.

THE AUTHOR

John Philip Newell is a poet, scholar, and teacher. The former warden of Iona Abbey in the Western Isles of Scotland, he is now companion theologian for the American Spirituality Center of Casa del Sol at Ghost Ranch in the high desert of New Mexico. Newell is internationally acclaimed for his work in the field of Celtic spirituality, including his much admired *Listening for the Heartbeat of God* and his poetic book of prayer, *Praying with the Earth*. He is a minister in the Church of Scotland with a passion for peace in the world and a fresh vision for harmony between the great spiritual traditions of humanity. A Canadian by birth, Newell maintains his family base in Edinburgh, Scotland, where he undertook his doctoral research in Celtic Christianity. On both sides of the Atlantic, he plays a leading role in the rebirthing of spirituality for today. For more information, visit his Web sites at www.johnphilipnewell.com and www.friendsofjohnphilipnewell.com.